MANAGING IRON SALESPEOPLE

HOW TO MANAGE SALESPEOPLE IN AN AGRICULTURAL DEALERSHIP

by Frank Lee

©2000, Sales Academy, Inc., Flower Mound, Texas. ALL RIGHTS RESERVED. No part of this book or any of its contents or collateral materials may be reproduced by any means or for any reason whatsoever without prior written permission from the holder of the copyright. No part of the content may be reproduced in whole or in part, stored in any retrieval system now known or to be known, transmitted in any form or by any means now known or to be known, photocopied by mechanical, electronic, or any other means now known or to be known, electronically recorded, or reproduced using technology now known or to be known, for any reason whatsoever, without prior written permission from the copyright holder.

Call Reluctance, the Fear-Free Prospecting and Self-Promotion Workshop and all related terms are copyrights and/or registered trade marks of Behavioral Sciences Research Press, Inc., Dallas Texas. Sales Academy is an Advanced Authorized Dealer for the Sales Call Reluctance program. ALL RIGHTS RESERVED. Used with permission.

ISBN # 0-9701399-2-6

Published by
Sales Academy Press
2628 Timberhaven Drive
Flower Mound, Texas, 75028
USA

1-800-898-3743
www.sales-academy.com

SALES ACADEMY, INC.
HELPING GOOD SALESPEOPLE BECOME BETTER

ACKNOWLEDGEMENTS

This was not an easy book to write. I worked on it for nearly two years before I was finally able to get it all down. A number of people helped me to complete it, some knowingly and others just by being there. I would like to acknowledge them and thank them.

Bill Fogarty, of Farm Equipment Magazine, gave up many hours of his precious time to edit it.

Bob Honzik, even in retirement from John Deere, provided me with advice that I could not get anywhere else.

Bob Hilleque, one of the best trainers I have ever met, acted as my mentor and continued to educate me.

A special thanks goes to Greg Goepferich of John Deere and Charlie Riley of AGCO. Their suggestions helped me name this book.

A number of people read my manuscript before publication and provided useful comments. Thank you - Jim Milstead of John Deere Company, Ron Tiller of Woods Manufacturing, Brian Hoven of Hoven Equipment in Montana, Craig Pottberg of Nebraska Machinery Company, Mark Nelson of Dakotaland Equipment in South Dakota, Jim Larson of Haug Implement in Minnesota, Dean Barnard of AGCO, Doug Griffin of Caterpillar, Mark Gettel of Gettels in Michigan, Todd Stucke of AGCO, and my colleagues in Singapore, Hock Seng Ong and Galen Chay. Some of their comments appear on the back of this book.

Heartfelt thanks go to the many dealers I have worked with over the years. I learned from them as I taught them. Everything I write about comes from my experiences with them. They were always willing to share information with me and provide me insights into this fascinating industry.

A big thank you goes to my wife, Pam, who still believes in me. She accepted my heavy travel schedule even when it disrupted her own career. She has encouraged me more than anyone. Finally, I must thank my two beautiful children, Ade and Dixi, for making me feel that they care about what I do. I hope they will approve of this book as much as they approved of my first!

CONTENTS

ACKNOWLEDGEMENTS

FOREWORD BY BILL FOGARTY

INTRODUCTION 1

CHAPTER 1 - WHAT IS A SALES MANAGER? 7
IS THERE A NEED FOR A FULL-TIME SALES
MANAGER IN A DEALERSHIP? 9
HOW TO TELL WHEN YOU NEED A SALES
MANAGER 9
HOW MANY PEOPLE CAN A SALES MANAGER
MANAGE EFFECTIVELY? 9
JOB DESCRIPTION OF THE SALES MANAGER 10
BEHAVIORAL ASPECTS OF SALES MANAGEMENT 14

CHAPTER 2 - SALES PHILOSOPHY 17
WHAT IS YOUR SALES PHILOSOPHY? 17
WHAT IS YOUR DEALERSHIP'S PHILOSOPHY? 19
WHAT IS YOUR PHILOSOPHY ON COMPETITORS? 20
REDUCE IT TO A CLEAR STATEMENT 21
WHO IS YOUR CUSTOMER AND WHAT DOES HE WANT? 22

CHAPTER 3 - TARGETS 25
WHAT ARE YOUR TARGETS? 25
MUST HAVE VS. LIKE TO HAVE VS. WILL GET 26
VALUE OF IDENTIFYING TARGETS REALISTICALLY 27
DEGREES OF COMMITMENT 28
ASSESSING DEALERSHIP SALES VOLUME
POTENTIAL 29
LONG-TERM ASSESSMENT 31
LOOK OUTSIDE THE BOX 32
OPPORTUNITY LISTENING 32
HOW MANY AND WHAT KIND OF SALESPEOPLE DO
YOU NEED? 33

WHAT TRAINING DO YOU NEED? 35

CHAPTER 4 - DEFINING A QUALITY SALE 37

CHAPTER 5 - ASSERTIVE MANAGEMENT 43
WHAT IS ASSERTIVE SALES MANAGEMENT? 44
WHY ASSERTIVE SALES MANAGEMENT? 44
HOW DO YOU BECOME ASSERTIVE? 46
SALES MANAGERS ALWAYS TEACH SALESPEOPLE 48

CHAPTER 6 - TERRITORIES 51
DEFINING A TERRITORY 52
ASSIGNING TERRITORIES 53
WORKING THE TERRITORY 54
SEGMENTING 54
DEVELOPING A STRATEGIC SALES PLAN 55
CALL FREQUENCIES 57
SALES MANAGER EXPECTATIONS 60
THE ROLE OF THE CSR 61

CHAPTER 7 - CUSTOMER SATISFACTION 63
THE CSI 63
CUSTOMER LOYALTY 64
PROFILES - KNOWING THE CUSTOMER 67
WHY SALESPEOPLE HATE PROFILES 68
HOW TO USE A PROFILE 69
DEVELOPING A FOLLOW THROUGH PROCESS 72

CHAPTER 8 - COMPETITION 75
WHAT SHOULD THE SALESPERSON LEARN ABOUT THE
COMPETITION? 76
HOW CAN A SALESPERSON FIND OUT? 77
COMPETITION PHILOSOPHY 79
WORKING WITH THE COMPETITION 80
INTEGRITY 81

CHAPTER 9 - WHY SALESPEOPLE FAIL 83
SACRED COWS AND OTHER HOLY SALESPEOPLE 86

CHAPTER 10 - SALES CALL RELUCTANCE 91
WHICH CALL RELUCTANCES AFFECT DEALERS MOST? 93
WHAT DOES THIS MEAN? 94
WHAT'S A SALES MANAGER TO DO? 97

CHAPTER 11 - DO YOU WANT SUPERSTAR SALESPEOPLE? 103
WHAT TO LOOK FOR 104
WHERE TO FIND SALESPEOPLE 105
THE INTERVIEW PROCESS 108
EARLY PERFORMANCE 108
CAREER PATHS 110

CHAPTER 12 - WHAT DO YOU EXPECT FROM YOUR SALESPEOPLE? 111
WHAT DO YOU WANT YOUR SALESPEOPLE TO DO? 111
CAN THEY DO IT? 113
NON-NEGOTIABLE BEHAVIORS 114
NON-NEGOTIABLE OR UNACCEPTABLE BEHAVIORS 115
SETTING GOALS 118

CHAPTER 13 - ESSENTIALS FOR SALESPEOPLE 123
1. GET TO KNOW THE CUSTOMER 123
2. PROFILES 124
3. KNOW THE COMPETITION 125
4. SELL THROUGH THE EYES OF THE CUSTOMER 126

CHAPTER 14 - MANAGING SUCCESSFUL BEHAVIORS 131
USING THE BEHAVIOR FORM 132
WHAT HAPPENS WHEN YOU FORGET? 133
P.A.S.S. C.A.L.F. - 8 BEHAVIORS OF SALES SUCCESS IN AN AGRICULTURAL DEALERSHIP 135

CHAPTER 15 - SALES TRAINING 141
FORMAL EDUCATION 142
TECHNOLOGY TRAINING 144
SELLING SKILLS 148

BEHAVIORAL SALES TRAINING 149
CONTINUOUS TRAINING 151
COACHING 154
SALES MEETINGS 156

CHAPTER 16 - LEADING THE SALES TEAM 159
THE SALES TEAM 163
MOTIVATING THE TEAM 164

CHAPTER 17 - SALESPERSON ACCOUNTABILITY 167
PLANNING SHEETS 168
PLANNING SHEET EXAMPLE 170
CALL REPORTS 171
EXAMPLE OF A CALL REPORT 172

CHAPTER 18 - EMPOWERING THE SALESPERSON 173
MICRO-MANAGEMENT 173
WHAT AND HOW MUCH AUTHORITY? 174
KNOW YOUR SALESPEOPLE 176

CHAPTER 19 - EVALUATING PERFORMANCE 177
WHY MEASURE? 178
WHAT TO MEASURE 179
MONTHLY REVIEWS 180
SALESPERSON REVIEWS 180

CHAPTER 20 - STRATEGIC SALES PLANNING 183
INCREASING EXISTING CUSTOMER SALES 183
ACQUIRING NEW MOST VALUED CUSTOMERS 186
DEVELOPING NEW MARKETS 188
USED EQUIPMENT 189

CHAPTER 21 - CREATING SUPERSTAR SALESPEOPLE 191

CHAPTER 22 - 8 SUCCESSFUL BEHAVIORS FOR SALES MANAGERS 193

CONCLUSION 195

ABOUT THE AUTHOR 197

FOREWORD

I did an article a few years ago for *Farm Equipment* magazine in which I pointed out that conditions were gradually worsening in the sales departments of agricultural machinery dealers. What made me such a know-it-all? I did a 20-year review of the annual Cost of Doing Business study put out by the North American Equipment Dealers Association. It provides operations data and balance sheet averages based on dealers reports.

You can't tell much just by comparing one year to another. But if you line up enough years' experience to show a major movement in dealers' operations, you have something approximating "proof."

So what did I prove? First, that gross margins on wholegoods sales had been declining consistently for two decades. No big surprise there -- anyone who's been in the game for even half that time knows it intuitively. But at least as important was this: The salaries of sales personnel as a percent of those gross margins had been increasing -- a bigger slice of a smaller pie!

While I was collecting data from those 20 years of dealer experience, I found myself giving a speech to a group of dealers in convention. I told them what I was smoking out -- slimmer margins, salespersons' income taking more of those margins -- and when I was finished talking, the dealer group president took the microphone and said, "Thanks, Bill. Looks like we need to go home and fire some of those salesmen of ours!"

I sat down, but I wish I had been nervy enough to grab the microphone back and say, "Actually, maybe you should go home and fire yourselves." I went back to my office and wrote an article about what my data indicated, along with my thoughts about what was at the root of the problem. And then I wrote my headline: *It's sales management, Dummy!* If I could have made that speech over again, that would have been its title.

A business expert I know once asked a room full of dealers, "What are the functions of sales management?" Everybody gave it a shot. "Correct pricing of trade-ins," "Training salesmen," "Planning promotional efforts," "Finding sales talent," and so on until the chalkboard was full. Then the expert said, "You're naming important functions, and there are many more. The more any and all of these are neglected, the more price becomes the overriding issue in every deal that comes up."

All the dealers I talked to after that session agreed that sales management was done on a haphazard basis just about everywhere in this business. Some of them admitted that they were still trying to do the job themselves and that there were just too many other demands on their time to do it right (even if they knew what to do). Others admitted that while they had a guy with the title of sales manager on their staffs, this was mostly an honorary thing bestowed on their best salesman, and if they made him a *real*, full-time manager, they'd lose volume. At least they seemed to understand that being a good salesman and being a good sales manager are different things.

Clearly, there are many equipment dealers out there who need some encouragement. They need to take the big step and establish a real sales manager position.

I wouldn't want to minimize either the need to get something going in this area or the enormity of the change such a move would entail.

But with the arrival of this book, I think the proper encouragement as well as the guidelines are finally at hand for any equipment dealer to draw on.

I only met Frank Lee a couple of years ago. He had been working with some dealers and the sales branches of a manufacturer. A lot of professional sales training consultants have done that, but this guy started riding around in pickup trucks with salespeople making calls. He was going home with dirty shoes every night, just like everyone else. He saw plenty about how sales work is done in this business -- the bad and the beautiful -- and he turned it into a book he titled *P.A.S.S. C.A.L.F. - 8 Behaviors of Sales Success in an Agricultural Dealership.* It had to do with the common behaviors of sales personnel on the job. It has sold well as dealers and salesmen have increasingly realized they need help.

Frank saw the huge sales management gap that exists out there. He felt that enough people in the equipment trade need some guidance, either in being a good sales manager or being a sales manager's boss, to make writing a book on it a worthwhile effort. He got the manuscript done and called this writer, asking me to put on my editor's cap and run over it with as sharp a pencil as I cared to wield.

For me, it was quite an honor. It was also very instructive. I never fully realized all the work, the opportunity and the reward that can go with the sales manager's job. Some of the things Frank wants a sales manager to do are not easy, but everything that can be done is a step in the right direction.

Is there a sales manager in any equipment dealership out there who's doing about everything that Frank brings up? Hey, show him/her to me. I'll want to meet this person -- and I'll want to meet his/her boss, who will be a dealer with a superior understanding of how this business works and what it takes to reach the potential that exists.

If you're the person who's got to manage a sales department, whatever else you may also have to do, read this book and note the steps you can perform with the least effort. Do them.

They'll make the next moves a little easier. I don't know how long it will take you to become a thorough professional in the position, but I know this: You have to start *now*.

Bill Fogarty
Editor Emeritus
Farm Equipment Magazine
2000

INTRODUCTION

In a sense, this book is like a Seinfeld episode – it is a book about nothing. This is not because the contents are "nothing" but because the position for which this book is written does not officially exist in most dealerships. Where it does exist on a titular basis only, the functions of sales management just don't get done.
Most dealers tell me they have a sales manager. He is usually the person who manages the salespeople, orders equipment, sells, and runs the dealership. Actually, his real title is store manager - but since you asked about a sales manager, there he is. He's somewhat harassed, often frazzled and quite concerned about his blood pressure. He performs his duties as well as he knows how and can proudly boast that he has led this

dealership to record sales and growth.

He is also well aware of his shortcomings and lack of formal training in the sales manager role. This becomes more apparent when you ask (as I have) many sales managers in dealerships to describe their roles in the dealership and to give their job descriptions. The answers vary widely enough to allow one to conclude that there is a certain amount of confusion. He is constantly on the lookout for things that can help make his job easier and more effective. He often becomes frustrated. Mostly it's because of the people aspect of sales management.

Salespeople, bless their hearts, can be the most frustrating people to manage. There is so much individualism – and ego! They tend to readily exploit weaknesses in sales managers. They are merciless when they sense they can get away with not doing what the sales manager politely requests. So many of the attributes that make them good salespeople also make them management nightmares. This is true in any industry. The salesperson in the dealership has one additional handicap – he has an ego larger than the dealership which is, for the most part, unearned and undeserved. This does not stop him from regularly reminding his manager that he is the one who really brings in the bread and butter of this dealership.

The sales manager tries everything to accommodate these super-egos, from cajoling to placating, begging and even pleading. Sometimes, he will explode, always to regret it later. What he fails to understand, however, is that most salespeople want to please him. That's true! Most salespeople actually would like to please their sales managers – if only they knew what their sales managers wanted and how they could please them. Many times the fault lies with the sales manager who has not made his expectations clear enough.

Then there are the superstar wannabes. They consistently

perform below expectations. They seem to consume more of the sales manager's time. They just never seem to be able to get it right. They make the worst deals and are always complaining about the lack of sales in their territories. They blame others, including the sales manager, for their lackluster performance. They drive the sales manager nuts but he cannot get rid of them. They bring in just enough to justify their presence in the dealership. And they have "potential"!

I have two observations on this. First, potential is for amateurs. Professionals bet on more substantial assets. Second, whenever a salesperson fails to deliver the goods, the first person to look to is the sales manager. Why? If a salesperson lacks certain skills or talents, the sales manager should have identified those deficiencies and trained for them. If he has, then the salesperson should improve. If a salesperson lacks motivation or goals, or is call reluctant, the sales manager should have provided the training and coaching necessary to eliminate these wasteful habits. If he did all this, he would not have salespeople who fail. What if he did and they still fail? The sales manager should have released them from the team. If they are still on the team, they are dragging the other members down and the ambivalent sales manager is allowing it to happen. This is why I always first look to the sales manager when there is a lack of performance in a sales team.

The harassed sales manager has to deal with all of these people problems in addition to managing inventory and placating suppliers who are constantly reminding him about unpleasant things like market share.

When asked about marketing plans and growth strategies, most sales managers in dealerships talk about their upcoming open day or their advertising efforts. They have not had time to do much more than that. Planning for the training and education of their salespeople is something that occurs whenever they get a

MANAGING IRON SALESPEOPLE

flyer or notification from their supplier about a new sales training program being offered in their area. That's when they think about how much it will cost and if can they afford to have the salesperson out of the field for another whole day.

If you're getting the picture that sales management in a dealership is not what it's supposed to be, you're right. This is hardly the fault of the sales manager. He has not been given the right tools or opportunities. Nor has he been given the time to devote to proper sales management. Most of the sales managers either own the dealerships or they were promoted to sales management based on skills that had nothing to do with management. Top salespeople regularly get promoted to sales managers. This assumes that, because they were able to sell well, they will be able to teach others how to sell and then get them to do it. This is a fatal assumption in many industries. The agricultural equipment industry is no different.

I have spent many hours with store/sales managers, salesperson/sales managers and the occasional genuine sales manager in dealerships. I learned to feel their pain as they pulled their hair out. I shared their frustrations when their salespeople defied their orders one more time and their joys when those same salespeople cracked big multi-unit deals. I agonized with them when a promising salesperson threatened to quit over a trivial incident. I felt their despair when they tried in vain to get their salespeople to complete all the paperwork on a deal. I watched as they swelled with pride when their salesperson converted a competitive owner cold call into a sale.

This book is written in two parts. The first part deals with the sales manager only. It deals with what I think a sales manager should be and some of the many duties of a sales manager. It explores the philosophies and beliefs of the individual sales manager and it talks about processes that will make his job easier. The second part shows him how to manage salespeople. Isn't this backwards? After all, my contention is that the main job of a sales manager is to manage salespeople. I deliberately wrote this book in the order I did because to be able to manage salespeople, the sales manager should first decide on some important career and business issues. Only when these have been clarified and documented can he effectively manage the people who will turn his dreams into reality. I urge the reader to start at the beginning and work his or her way through. After you have read through the book in its designed sequence, you can select pieces to read that may interest you.

This is not a novel. It is not as entertaining as that. This was written as a textbook for a sales manager workshop that I am developing. It will also serve as reference material for the sales manager of the dealership of the future.

Talking of the dealership of the future, one must recognize that the growing number of competent females entering this industry will bring a new dimension and outlook. I acknowledge this trend and applaud it. I have met many female managers who perform admirably. In this book I refer to sales manager and salesperson as "he" because that is generally the way it is right now. Also, it makes easier reading. This is not disparaging to the female population. All references to males apply equally to females.

For the purist sales manager – this is not a Harvard Business School thesis. There are many good managers in dealerships who would benefit from getting an MBA but will never have the time or opportunity to do so. This does not mean that they will never be able to manage a sales team. While parts of this book may appear basic and even childishly simple, I make no apologies for this. For years, I have taught managers "down-and-dirty" management practices. I have never been interested in the theories and neither have the managers I have taught. I have always only been interested in two things for managers – get

MANAGING IRON SALESPEOPLE

your people to do what you need them to do and keep improving them. My belief has always been that, if you do these two things, you will succeed as a manager. If you don't, then all the theories don't matter and you are a manager in name only.

No matter how good a salesperson the sales manager is, no matter how hard he works, no matter how many hours he puts in, he will never be able to sell all the iron in his dealership. For that, he relies on salespeople. Getting them to do it, do it in huge numbers, and do it with a smile is every sales manager's dream. Perhaps this book will help get you closer to that dream.

CHAPTER 1 - WHAT IS A SALES MANAGER?

Those who have been in sales or sales management, and who loved it, tend to get sentimental when asked about a good sales manager. Or they become vindictive when talking about a bad one. They will tell you that he or she is someone who motivates others, inspires salespeople, supports them, listens to them and generally puts their welfare ahead of everyone else's. One often hears the term, "He goes to bat for me."

Salespeople differ in their descriptions of a good sales manager. These can range from "he leaves me alone" to "he's always looking over my shoulder." The thing that comes up most in describing a good sales manager, however, is that he or she cares for me. This is not a surface caring but rather a deep, genuine caring for the development of the salesperson. The best sales managers genuinely care about their salespeople. This does not mean letting them get away with murder. Rather, like good parents, they want their salespersons to do well and to have the opportunities to achieve their potential. Once this genuine caring is present, most of the sales manager's direction falls into place.

Perhaps this is a good time to explore what behaviors make a good sales manager. I use the term "behaviors" because it really

MANAGING IRON SALESPEOPLE

doesn't matter what qualities a sales manager has if he does not do the right things consistently.

Here are some of the things a good sales manager should do on a consistent basis.

1. Care about each salesperson.
2. Get salespeople to do the behaviors that will make them successful.
3. Constantly train, coach and develop the salespeople as individuals.
4. Constantly develop the sales team.
5. Provide on-going product knowledge to make the salespeople the most knowledgeable in the industry.
6. Assertively manage them.
7. Support them in issues, but seldom at the expense of the company or the customer.
8. Expect the best of them and make sure they know what those expectations are.
9. Set very high standards for himself.
10. Create a success environment where salespeople can feel excitement.
11. Understand that he is judged by the success of his salespeople, nothing else.

Does this sound like a full-time job? You bet it does! This is why part-time sales managers find it so difficult to be truly effective. Can it be done? There are thousands of very good sales managers all over the world who are already doing this and more. Can it be done in a dealership? Yes, but the owner of the dealership must understand the importance of a full-time sales manager and support him. Will this happen soon? It is already happening in some of the larger, more progressive dealerships.

IS THERE A NEED FOR A FULL-TIME SALES MANAGER IN A DEALERSHIP?

Except in cases where the dealership is a very small mom-and-pop operation, the answer is a resounding yes. This applies to all size dealerships, even those that feel they cannot afford a full-time sales manager now. A full-time sales manager in a dealership should always be able to generate more profitable sales through others than he costs.

HOW TO TELL WHEN YOU NEED A SALES MANAGER

If the following conditions can be met, you need a full-time sales manager:
1. You have 2 or more full-time salespeople.
2. You are operating at 50% or lower market share and you can get more.
3. Your salespeople tell you that they cannot possibly do more sales.
4. Your salespeople are habitually running the same trap lines.
5. Your sales campaigns are ineffective or nonexistent.
6. Your sales are not as profitable as the industry norms.

HOW MANY PEOPLE CAN A SALES MANAGER MANAGE EFFECTIVELY?

The answer to this depends on the sales manager himself. The accepted norm is 10 salespeople. However, I know of some excellent sales managers that manage 30 or more salespeople. I even know of a sales manager who has 50 salespeople on his team and they regularly thump the competition.

In large, multi-store operations, it is preferable to have one overall sales manager who has store sales managers reporting to him. In smaller multi-store operations, one sales manager should be sufficient. However, this depends on the distance between stores and whether the sales manager can get all of the salespeople together reasonably easily. Logistics play a major role. If the distance between stores is too great to allow for regular sales meetings that all salespeople can attend, then a sales manager per region may be advisable.

Since most dealerships do not have more than 10 salespeople, the general answer is that one sales manager should be able to do an effective job.

JOB DESCRIPTION OF THE SALES MANAGER

Each store location will have a specific job description for the sales manager. Here are some guidelines.

1. The sales manager should be responsible for all wholegoods sales in a dealership. This includes new wholegoods, used wholegoods and dealership programs.
2. The sales manager should be responsible for the development of the sales team. This includes education, training and general development.
3. The sales manager should be responsible for the activities of the sales team. This includes directing them, assigning territories, developing successful behaviors for them, disciplining them, rewarding them and defining non-negotiable

behaviors - and enforcing them.
4. The sales manager should hire and fire salespeople. The sales manager should also be responsible for setting the wage and commission scales for the salespeople and should develop an equitable reward system.
5. The sales manager should develop budgets for the sales department and be responsible for creating advertising, special promotions and other promotional events.
6. The sales manager should liaise with suppliers and negotiate the best terms and deals with these suppliers.
7. The sales manager should take on new lines when appropriate for the market, source such new lines and negotiate the best terms.
8. The sales manager should examine the trade area of the dealership, ensure that the dealership is properly represented in this area and is receiving the appropriate amount of business from it.
9. The sales manager should uncover new markets and develop strategies for exploiting them.
10. The sales manager should coordinate the efforts of all departments to maximize any promotions or other opportunities for the dealership.
11. The sales manager should regularly communicate the strategies of the sales department to other employees.
12. The sales manager should set targets for the sales department and for each individual salesperson and be responsible for achieving them.
13. The sales manager should liaise with customers when the salesperson is unable to complete a sale or when there is a problem.
14. The sales manager should ensure that all paperwork is completed in the approved manner and should create the correct paperwork where this is insufficient or lacking.

MANAGING IRON SALESPEOPLE

15. The sales manager should create sales systems to ensure the proper procedures are followed in the making of sales. This includes developing a proper follow-up system after each sale.
16. The sales manager should create incentive schemes for the salespeople, the sales department and other departments with the cooperation of the other managers. This should include contests.
17. The sales manager should be responsible for the upkeep and maintenance of the dealer sales vehicles and any other equipment under the control of the sales department.
18. The sales manager should report on a regular basis to the owner of the dealership. He should be accountable to the owner, a board or silent partner (if he is also the owner) for his actions and for sales results.
19. The sales manager should develop a one-year and a five-year business plan for the sales department, have it approved by the general manager and meet regularly with the general manager to review this plan. The sales manager should also share this business plan with the sales team on a regular basis.
20. The sales manager should formulate policies in the sales department. This includes trade-in policies, new color conversion policies, hours that salespeople are available, sales policies, training policies and any other appropriate policies.
21. The sales manager should develop a sales philosophy for the dealership and ensure that all salespeople are aware of this philosophy and follow it in their dealings with customers. He should also develop a competitor philosophy.
22. The sales manager should hold regular sales meetings with all salespeople.
23. The sales manager should promote the dealership at every

opportunity. This includes joining and participating in community or civic organizations.
24. The sales manager should develop a one-year training and education plan for each individual salesperson. He should also develop one for himself.
25. The sales manager should set an example for the salespeople and the rest of the dealership by arriving at work on time, leaving at the appropriate time, keeping appointments, respecting the time of others and generally behaving in a manner appropriate for a professional.
26. The sales manager should attend all management meetings and be prepared to contribute at each one.
27. The sales manager should be aware of all developments in the industry as well as all training opportunities for the salespeople and himself.
28. The sales manager should keep abreast of all new equipment from the dealer's suppliers as well as all competitive equipment.
29. The sales manager should always be up-to-date on pricing practices in the dealer trade area as well as those in adjacent areas.
30. The sales manager should compile a library of literature, videotapes and other materials helpful to the salespeople. These should include competitive equipment.
31. The sales manager should be aware of what competitors are doing and should regularly formulate strategies to beat them.
32. The sales manager should always be aware of the inventory of the dealership, both new and used, and make every effort to develop plans for moving this inventory.
33. In multi-store operations, the sales manager should be aware of inventory on all dealership lots and make sure this information is available to all salespeople.
34. The sales manager should constantly be updating his and

MANAGING IRON SALESPEOPLE

the salespeople's knowledge of the customers of the dealership. This includes the collecting of profiles, updating them and analyzing them.
35. The sales manager should examine ways to educate the customers of the dealership.
36. The sales manager should coordinate and lead events such as customer clinics, open days, customer focus group meetings and the attending of trade shows.
37. The sales manager should foster cooperation between the sales and other departments.
38. The sales manager should maintain an open-door policy for all salespeople and managers.
39. If a dealership has a lawn and grounds care department, the sales manager should be responsible for the sales side of this department and should apply all of the above to this department as well.

Does this still sound like a part-time job? Consider this – if you had one person who could do all of the above, how much additional business could you bring in? As comprehensive a list as this is, I'll bet there are some dealers who could add to it.

If you are a sales manager in a dealership, I'll bet your duties were not explained to you in so much detail. What you have to ask yourself is this – am I doing all of the above to my own satisfaction?

BEHAVIORAL ASPECTS OF SALES MANAGEMENT

Besides the job description, the sales manager should have some very clear behavioral expectations. Rather than repeat some of the above, I have added the following:

1. At every sales meeting, include some form of sales training.
2. Plan your days well.
3. Spend a minimum of 5 hours each week updating your knowledge of your industry, your customers and the competition. Set this time aside in your planning.
4. Travel with each salesperson on at least one sales call per week. Use this sales call to coach the salesperson to become better at selling.
5. Spend one day each quarter working on your best customer's farm and make sure your salespeople do the same.
6. Spend one day each quarter working in the other dealer departments and make sure your salespeople do the same.
7. After each training session, make sure your salespeople do the follow-up exercises and make sure you see evidence of the training in their activities following every workshop.
8. Manage consistently, fairly and assertively.
9. Support your fellow managers.
10. Maintain open and consistent communication with all departments.
11. Attend, as a participant, every sales class that your salespeople attend.
12. Maintain a high work ethic and insist on the same from each salesperson.
13. Set high standards for yourself and lead your salespeople to adopt these high standards.
14. Get rid of salespeople who cannot be helped – fast.
15. Develop teams involving the other departments. Salespeople should lead these teams and each team should have a specific goal such as the acquiring of a specific high-volume prospect.
16. Constantly find new ways to make the dealership an attrac-

tive and fun place to work.

Sounds like a fun job, doesn't it? It is, or it can be. This is why it is important to have the right person in the job. Who is the right person? This depends on many things including the personality of the dealer principal. It is very seldom the best salesperson in the dealership. It requires someone who is well educated, resourceful and willing to learn. This person should already have some leadership abilities but not be cocky enough to think he already knows it all. This person should be empathetic but not wimpy. Assertion is important. A solid work ethic is a must. An ability to think ahead and to see the bigger picture is very helpful. Someone who genuinely cares about people is paramount.

How much will he cost? Strangely enough, he is already costing you. If you do not have someone like this in your dealership, you are already paying for him in terms of lost sales and opportunities.

Depending on location and size, his wages could be anything from $40,000 to $100,000 per year plus overriding commissions. Can't afford him? Do your math. How much additional business can someone like him bring into your dealership that you don't already have? Is it two more tractors a year? Twenty? How many additional gross margin dollars will be there from wholegoods sales - because his work helped to hold the price line? When you have made that calculation, the net amount should exceed his salary plus 50%. After all, you do want to make a profit, don't you?

CHAPTER 2 - SALES PHILOSOPHY

From this point, I will be writing as if I were writing to the sales manager in a dealership. I will address you, the reader, as the sales manager. If you are not, then pretend you are, because you are obviously looking for some sales management advice or you would not be reading this.

WHAT IS YOUR SALES PHILOSOPHY?

Before you can effectively manage a sales team, you must determine what your sales philosophy is. You must be able to state it clearly and communicate it to your dealership, particularly the sales team.

What is a sales philosophy? It's how you view the whole sales process. It's also basically how you would like to be treated if you were the customer.

Some sales managers view selling as a game. They want to have fun at it. They create fun environments, keep upbeat even when they're losing the game and inspire their salespeople to be happy no matter what.

MANAGING IRON SALESPEOPLE

Some sales managers view selling as an "us versus them" struggle. They are constantly trying to outwit the customer and encourage salespeople to do the same. They don't mind little white lies as long as they get the sale. Getting the sale is all-important. While they would like long-term customer loyalty, it is more important to make the numbers today. They will do whatever it takes to get a sale.

Some sales managers view selling as a relationship. They feel the long-term good of the business is better served by having loyal and repeat customers and they encourage their salespeople to develop lasting relationships with their customers. They will occasionally bend the rules in favor of this relationship and may even trade badly at times as long as the relationship is not disturbed.

Some sales managers view selling as a business. They view the sales department as a profit center and, although they want every piece of business they can get, they are prepared to walk away from unprofitable business. They care about the needs of the customer, but they are always concerned for the financial well being of their business.

Some sales managers view selling as a necessary evil. They secretly wish that they did not have to have salespeople and that customers could make their own buying decisions. They would feel more comfortable selling from a catalog or over the Internet.

Some sales managers view selling as a professional occupation where the needs of the customer come ahead of the business. They meet and exceed the expectations of their customers. They constantly spend time learning about the needs of the customer and find creative ways to meet those needs. Their concept of a long-term relationship is one where both parties' needs are met and both parties are willing participants in this relationship. They train their salespeople to go beyond the standards of their competitors. Some sales managers have a mixture of some or all of the above. They balance profit with relationships and instant sales with long-term objectives. And then there are those who use bits of each depending on the occasion. They manage by circumstance, consider themselves flexible and often confuse their salespeople.

It is very important that you start with a well-thought-out selling philosophy. Your salespeople will mimic you and will carry on your legacy even after you have retired. This is one of the most important things you can leave behind in a dealership. What is your selling philosophy?

WHAT IS YOUR DEALERSHIP'S PHILOSOPHY?

It is very important to match your selling philosophy with that of the dealership. If the rest of the dealership operates on a selling philosophy vastly different to yours, you will constantly be compromising, arguing and generally going in opposite directions.

How can you tell what the selling philosophy of a dealership is? Look at its pattern of behaviors in selling to various customers. How consistent has it been? Most dealers talk a good game but many have not even formulated a coherent selling philosophy. Many shoot from the hip, letting circumstances dictate the selling philosophy of the day.

If there is no consistent selling philosophy in your dealership, perhaps you can create one. Make sure that this is fully understood by the dealer principal and that he buys into it and is prepared to support it. This support should have behavioral implications and not simply be lip service. Get it in writing, if necessary. Whenever there is a discrepancy in the selling philosophies of the sales manager and the dealership, the sales manager usually ends up losing his job. Sometimes he quits through sheer frustration. Sometimes he gets fired because he is unable to reconcile this difference with the owners.

The ideal is to have the two philosophies match. This makes your job as sales manager easier and provides a clear and concise direction for the entire dealership. Salespeople and all other employees are not left to guess. They know exactly where you and the dealership stand on this vital issue.

WHAT IS YOUR PHILOSOPHY ON COMPETITORS?

This should also be clearly defined and should match that of your dealership. I have witnessed two opposing ends of the spectrum on this, as well as all the shades in between.

In one dealership, the philosophy was a live and let live one. In fact, they would go out of their way to avoid confrontation with the competitive dealer. They would walk away from sales that the opposing dealer was involved in, claiming that he would do the same. I'm not sure if he did or not. Perhaps he did and they lived in peaceful coexistence.

In another dealership, competition was another story altogether. There were three dealerships in town. All three hated each other. They would do whatever it took to steal business from each other. While this created a healthy competitive market for the farmer, none of them operated on high enough margins to properly service what they sold. I witnessed some dirty and underhanded tactics to beat the other dealer in a trade. Profit was secondary to winning senseless battles. Emotion overruled business sense.

Then, of course, there are the many shades between. Very few are as clear-cut as these two examples. However, you should have a clear-cut philosophy. This makes it easier for your salespeople to deal with competition in the way you would like them to do. They won't have to second-guess you.

One of the best philosophies I ever found in a dealership came from Ohio. The dealer there, a multi-store operation, stated very simply: "We're the best. We're better than our competition. We have better facilities, equipment, people and operations. Therefore, we want the best customers. We don't mind him being in our trade area and we welcome him. But, when it comes to the top customers, we can service them better than he can and, therefore, we deserve them."

This left no doubt in the minds of his salespeople that they should proudly stand up to competition, win deals by delivering more, not cutting prices, and that they deserved the best customers. Guess what? The opposing dealer readily accepted the role of the underdog and did nothing to change it. It is now de-facto in this area that there is one outstanding dealer and one also-ran. Guess who the top customers migrate to?

REDUCE IT TO A CLEAR STATEMENT

Once you have formulated your philosophies on selling and the competition, reduce them to one simple, clear statement. Avoid the mistake that many companies make in developing their mission statements. Keep it simple and understandable. Make sure all your salespeople can repeat it. Make sure everyone in the dealership can repeat it. Make it a part of your training. Make sure all training provided to your salespeople builds on this philosophy. Reject anything that does not.

Make sure all your salespeople live it.

TWO MISSION STATEMENTS

Have you ever gone into an executive's office and seen the company mission statement on the wall in an expensive-looking frame? I have and I have read many of them.

Three things have struck me.
1. Almost all of them use abstract, flowery language.
2. After reading it, I still did not know exactly what the company was supposed to do.
3. They all sounded the same. Do all companies get their mission statements from the same factory?

Some companies display their mission statements all over their places of business. Perhaps this is to remind the employees of how clever the marketing department is. Or, is it the president? I have very seldom seen customers reading these mission statements.

All mission statements say two basic things no matter what language they use — we want to be the best and we want to make our customers happy. Both are admirable targets to strive for. However, the behaviors of the employees tell a different mission statement. The behaviors often say things like, "We don't really care about our customers and being mediocre is good enough for us."

WHO IS YOUR CUSTOMER AND WHAT DOES HE WANT?

Let's ask ourselves: Who exactly is your customer and what does he want?

Many sales managers forget that their real customer is

the *salesperson*. Just because they have the title of sales manager does not mean that the salesperson they manage will automatically buy into everything they say. You have to constantly be selling your ideas to your salespeople, even after you have been on the job many years. Many managers believe that their salespeople will do whatever they are told to do. This may be true in some departments. In the case of salespeople, they have this annoying tendency to question authority. This means you. Some may even be convinced that you make mistakes occasionally or that you did not think that last memo through properly. They may even be right.

Once you have achieved credibility with your salespeople, selling your ideas comes easier. But it is always there. Incidentally, credibility comes with time. Until you have it, be a better salesperson yourself.

How do you sell your ideas to salespeople? The same way you would sell to any other customer! Look at things through the eyes of your customer. If you were the salesperson, what would convince you to make another cold call? Or collect a profile? Ask yourself, "What does he want and how can doing this help to move him closer to getting what he wants?" Then help him achieve his dreams and both of you can win.

What do salespeople want? There is no clear answer on this. The obvious answers are not always correct. More sales, easier sales, more money, less work, less stress, guaranteed sales. Perhaps one or more of these apply to your salesperson. Perhaps not.

It's dangerous to make assumptions when it comes to salespeople. There are too many individuals in this group. You could ask but you may get the stock answers. Here are some questions that may just elicit a more honest response:

"If you could change one thing in this dealership that

would make your job better, what would that be?"
"How would that help the customer?"
"Why would that help the customer?"
"If you wanted to make the customer feel better about doing more business with you, what would you change in yourself?"
"Why? How would that help?"
"What would you like to do more of for customers that you are not currently doing?"
"What prevents this from happening?"

There is one thing all salespeople want (and I defy you to bring me a salesperson who doesn't) – respect. One of the biggest thrills a salesperson can experience is when the customer regards him as his consultant. The customer calls him first before making any purchasing decision. The customer calls for advice. Salespeople are constantly striving to reach this level with their customers. Help your salespeople get there and you may have a very receptive audience for your ideas.

CHAPTER 3 - TARGETS

Setting realistic targets for each salesperson and the entire sales department is essential. These targets become the focus of all efforts in the dealership. They give direction to the sales team and provide a measuring stick for success.

WHAT ARE YOUR TARGETS?

Often, when I ask dealers what their sales targets are for the next 12 months, I get vague answers. Some respond by saying they would be happy to do what they did last year. When asked how much they did the previous year, some are not sure. They need to look it up. True managers know what they did last year and know the exact target for the next year. There is very little guesswork involved. Some managers use the "PFA" (pluck from air) method of selecting targets. They respond with a 10% or 20% increase but have no idea what this involves.

There has to be an overall sales target. This overall sales target should be quantifiable in money terms that can be broken down. "Our sales for the next 12 months should be $14 million, a 10% increase on last year's wholegoods sales. To achieve this, we must sell x number of combines, x number of 4-wheel-drive tractors, and so on." This shows a more methodical approach to targets.

In order to set realistic sales targets, the sales manager must know the following:

1. How much we did last year and how we achieved it.
2. What is the farming outlook for the next year?
3. How much additional business is available in our trade area?
4. What resources do we have available?
5. What additional resources can we count on this year?

Once the above are answered satisfactorily and in some detail, the sales manager can set a realistic overall sales target for the next year. He can also forecast targets for the following three to four years.

Having set these targets, he must now look at how to achieve them. He must break the overall target down into smaller targets.

1. Numbers of units of different brands, sizes, new and used, and so on.
2. Monthly or quarterly targets.
3. Behavioral targets. What behaviors do my salespeople need to do to accomplish this?

MUST HAVE VS. LIKE TO HAVE VS. WILL GET

At this stage, he must determine what he must have in order for the department to survive. This becomes the "bottom-line" target, the minimum that has to be accomplished. He should have a basic plan on how to do this.

He should also look at what he would ideally like to have. This is the "top-end" target, what he will shoot for.

Finally, he must look at what he will realistically get regardless of any other factors. This is the "steady-business" target that he should be able to count on. He can then plan on how to make sure these sales do not somehow slip away during the year.

With these three numbers, he can formulate a game plan with a plan B.

VALUE OF IDENTIFYING TARGETS REALISTICALLY

"PFA" target setting is for amateurs. Professional managers know that one should always set realistic targets based on the factors listed above. Why? Unrealistically optimistic targets tend to demoralize salespeople when they are unable to reach them. Worse, they begin to develop the habit of not reaching targets. They lose faith in the sales manager and ultimately disregard all targets as pie in the sky.

Unrealistically low targets have the same effect but for different reasons. There is no longer a challenge. Targets become so easy to achieve that salespeople stop taking them seriously. Worse, they achieve them and nothing else! Salespeople often tend to do just enough. Ask them to make three sales and they will. Ask for four and they will, too. Perhaps you should have asked for four in the first place.

Realistic targets are based on proper analysis rather than shooting from the hip. It requires thought, research, analysis and clear thinking. This is what a sales manager is hired to do.

DEGREES OF COMMITMENT

Once the targets are set, the sales manager should develop a clear plan to achieve those targets. One of the things he must realize is that he will not reach those targets without something *new* being done. This requires some change from his salespeople. If he does nothing different, he will either get the same results as last year or he will go backwards. However, change is often not easy for salespeople to accept and embrace. It usually means that they will be doing more work. The good sales manager understands this and gets a strong commitment from his salespeople by selling them on his plan.

There are four degrees of commitment.

1. The first says, "I don't want to change." This is actually a very strong commitment and one that will sabotage the sales plan before you start.
2. The second says, "I would like to change and I'll try." This is a wimpish sort of commitment that usually does not yield many results.
3. The third says, "I want to change and I'll do my best." This is a stronger form of commitment. However, it still is set for failure because it means I'll give up if my best is not enough.
4. The fourth says, "I want to change and I will do whatever it takes." This is the highest form of commitment because it does not allow for failure or excuses.

The sales manager should assess where all of his salespeople are in terms of commitment to change and to their careers. He should try to sell them on giving the fourth degree of commitment but he should also realistically know where each one really is. This will determine the amount of behavioral management that will be needed. This is a resource and so it should be added to the resource mix.

Incidentally, the sales manager who starts out without himself having this fourth degree of commitment *already has an enemy in his camp.*

ASSESSING DEALERSHIP SALES VOLUME POTENTIAL

For the sales manager to realistically set targets, he should know what the sales volume potential is for his dealership in his trade area. How does he do this?

There are a number of trade resources that manufacturers provide on market share. These evaluate the numbers of the different types of equipment that have been sold in the area and estimate the numbers that can be sold. This is a good start. However, it falls short of properly analyzing the territory. The sales manager should do this.

Segmenting is a useful tool. The sales manager should break up his total trade area into manageable segments and then assign one salesperson to one segment at a time. Using plat maps and simple "eyeball" prospecting, the salesperson should first plot the locations of the dealer's existing customers. Then he should identify all possible prospects in the same segment and plot them on the segmented map. This will identify as much as possible every potential customer for the dealership in that segment.

Once this is done, the salesperson does the same for the next segment and so on until the entire trade area has been covered.

The value of segmenting is that it focuses the salesperson on a small area. When asked to do this for an entire trade area, it becomes overwhelming and salespeople give up early and the job never gets completed. One small segment is more manageable.

After all possible prospects are identified, the sales manager can proceed in one of two ways. He can quickly assess the prospects or he can do so over time.

To do so over time, he would list the names of each customer in each segment and then list the names of each prospect on either side of that customer. The list would look like this.

SEGMENT ONE		
Prospect	**Customer**	**Prospect**
Ramona's Farm	Hidge Farm	Jerry & Mary White
Ong Brothers	Fleetwood Farm	The Lincoln's
Wilson Farms	Galen's Farms	Jack Hajibey, Inc.
Merlin, Inc.		

Now, each time a salesperson calls on one of the customers, he is expected to automatically call on the prospects on either side of that customer. This becomes a systematic method of getting to know every single prospect in your trade area. The sales manager should insist on a report from the salesperson after each such call.

The salesperson's objectives for calling on the prospects are first to qualify them as either prospects or not, and to make sure that the person or persons know about the dealership whether or not they are true prospects. This will help set up a proper prospect base for further calling or have the name removed from the segment map.

To do this in a hurry, the sales manager should circulate a list of all the prospects to everyone in the dealership. If anyone knows the person or farm, they should indicate this on the list. The sales manager can then follow up with the person in the dealership to gather additional information that will label the person either as a prospect or have the name removed.

For the remaining names, the sales manager should send the salespeople out specifically to call on these people. This can be done in the off-season. Each salesperson will have one segment to cover. He is to call on each name to introduce himself and to assess the business potential of the prospect.

The idea is to collect enough data so that the sales manager can reasonably assess the value of business available in his trade area as well as the numbers of prospects his salespeople will have to convert to customers.

Note to sales managers – don't fall into the trap salespeople sometimes lay. They will tell you that everyone in the trade area has done business with the dealership in the past, is currently doing business with the dealership, or at least knows about the dealership. In other words, we know who's out there and there is no need for us to do this useless exercise. Get them to do the useless exercise anyway. You may be surprised at how many people in your area do not know you. Your salespeople may be too.

LONG-TERM ASSESSMENT

Based on what you know and what you can realistically expect, you should now be able to assess how much wholegoods business you can get in the next year. You should also be able to forecast two years and even five years out. Some sales managers have told me this is not possible because of the uncertainty of factors like the weather. I say plan anyway. You can always adjust your plan if conditions change on you. Letting factors like the weather stop you from planning at all is a very providential attitude. You can bet that companies like Deere, Caterpillar, Agco and Case plan well into the future and they are subjected to the same conditions that affect your market.

As a side note – you should make use of the resources offered by your supplier to help you plan. They have experts available who would be very happy to share their expertise with an interested sales manager.

LOOK OUTSIDE THE BOX

In assessing sales volume potential, look outside the box. Today, there are many non-agricultural applications for agricultural equipment. I often do an exercise with both dealers and manufacturer territory managers. I ask them to think of one application for their equipment that is not the usual one, a use they think no others in the group will think of. After they have written down their thoughts, we go around the room and each person responds. I am always amazed at how creative people become in this situation. They will not only identify a different application, they will identify the industry to which this application would apply and even names of companies in this industry.

Perhaps you should do the same in your dealership.

One example – the weekend farmer is a growing, viable market. I predict that, someday, a savvy dealer is going to specialize in this market and make a fortune.

OPPORTUNITY LISTENING

Opportunity listening simply means listening for opportunities. It has two practical applications. First, it means listening for opportunities for your sales team. Second, it means listening for opportunities for your customers.

You practice opportunity listening for your customers when you are always listening for ways to help them do their business better. In discussions with your customers, pretend that you are on their board of directors and every meeting is a board meeting. How can you help them do better business?

You practice opportunity listening for your sales team when you are always listening and looking for different markets for them.

Get into the habit of opportunity listening and you may be surprised at how many business opportunities you will come across.

OPPORTUNITY LISTENING THE WRONG WAY

We have all practiced opportunity listening at some time. I remember as a teenager how I used to gaze into a young girl's eyes and devote my full attention to her. She thought I was the most attentive person she had ever met. *I was simply listening for opportunities.* I guess that is the third practical application. Unfortunately, I had not perfected it back then so it did not help me.

HOW MANY AND WHAT KIND OF SALESPEOPLE DO YOU NEED?

Once you have uncovered your market potential, you may find that you do not have enough salespeople to fully exploit this market or you may be limited by the quality of the salespeople you do have. Neither is a reason to give up on the market.

If you do not have enough salespeople, start looking for additional ones. Your dealership may not be willing to spend the extra amount on another salesperson for a number of legitimate business reasons. Therefore, you should do your homework well before suggesting this.

How do you know when you need another salesperson? Whenever you have evidence that your current salespeople are leaving a lot of deals on the table, you may need another salesperson. I once traveled with the salespeople of a dealership. Each morning, I would meet with the owner of the dealership before going out with his salespeople. After a few days, he asked me, "What do you think of my salespeople?" He was proud of them for good reason. They were regularly bringing in millions of dollars of sales. So, he was somewhat surprised at my answer. I told him, "Even with my limited knowledge of farm equipment, I could make a living off the sales your salespeople leave behind. All I would have to do is follow them and pick up the scraps they discard and I would earn a living." I had witnessed them driving by large farms. When asked why, they dismissed the farmer as somebody who does not buy. I had seen them follow up too late or not at all and lose deals as a result. Is this happening in your dealership? If it is, and your salespeople are still producing big numbers, it may be time for another salesperson.

What type of salesperson do you need? This depends on the market you're looking at. One thing I know for sure – you cannot hire salespeople the way dealers have traditionally done for years. The market has changed, become more sophisticated. One dealer in Montana said he would never hire a salesperson again that did not have a college degree. I tend to agree with him. If you're looking at the corporate farming market, you will need someone who has the ability to penetrate that market. If your market is government, you will need a salesperson adept in this market. If your market is the weekend farmer, you may need a salesperson who is able to communicate well at this level and who is willing and able to become a valuable resource for the weekend farmer.

What if your salespeople don't meet your needs? You should assess each one individually to see if there is room for improvement. If there is not, you should seriously assess whether or not he can still be a valuable team member. If there is, you should immediately start looking for the right training to properly equip him for the markets you are assigning him.

There is a lot of sales training available. However, you should properly assess your training needs and select only the sales training that will accomplish what you want. This training should be very specific for your industry and your market.

WHAT TRAINING DO YOU NEED?

The good sales manager is always looking for ways to improve his own skills. Look at training programs offered by your manufacturer, although these may be rare. Manufacturers have not always provided this type of training. Traditionally, this has not been needed. One exception is an outstanding program provided by John Deere and taught by my good friend, Bob Hilleque. It's called "Coaching for Commitment" and provides sales managers with some useful management tools.

If your manufacturer does not provide the right sales management training, look outside. There are consultants that can provide it. Sales Academy, for example, provides valuable sales management training in its Successful Dealer Behaviors Program.

There are colleges that have excellent sales management programs.

MANAGING IRON SALESPEOPLE

Join organizations like SME (Sales and Marketing Executives) which has a sales management certification course. They also provide monthly networking meetings and usually have very good speakers who often bring practical advice. If you're lucky enough to live in an area where they have a chapter, you should join.

There are also organizations like AMA (American Management Association), though I have not seen anything they offer that would be of practical use to the sales manager in a dealership. I may be wrong. Check them out though and make up your own mind.

Of course, there are numerous books on sales management and leadership that can help.

There is training available. It is up to the professional sales manager to find it, evaluate it for practicality and then use it.

CHAPTER 4 - DEFINING A QUALITY SALE

Far too many dealerships struggle with this problem. What is a quality sale for a dealership?

The best answer that I received from one dealer is a sale that provides better than average margin without a trade-in, locks the customer in for future parts and service sales and makes the customer happy. If only it were this simple!

Very often there is a trade and this need not be a bad thing. After all, dealers need used equipment to round out their businesses. In this case, according to the above definition, the trade should ideally have a home before it hits the lot, or it should have reasonable prospects of finding a home. It should also be traded in at a price that allows for additional profit after it is sold.

My definition of a quality sale is far simpler. It is one where both parties benefit. The farmer should receive the best equipment for his needs at a reasonable price. The dealer should make a reasonable profit.

Therefore, according to my definition, the first thing to look at is the need of the customer. Sometimes, a customer will come into a dealership and ask about a certain type of equipment.

MANAGING IRON SALESPEOPLE

The salesperson automatically goes into the sales pitch about that piece of equipment and the conversation invariably turns to price. The salesperson assumes that the farmer knows exactly what he wants and is simply shopping prices. What if the farmer is not shopping prices but options? What if he genuinely is not sure which piece of equipment will be the best for his application?

Would it not benefit both the farmer and the dealership if the salesperson were to simply ask, "What are you going to do with this?" and then lead the farmer into the right equipment based on his specific needs?

I wish this had been the case when I bought computer equipment for my business. I went into one computer store after another, hoping to find someone who would take the time to discover my needs. Each time, the computer salesperson would immediately begin selling me something that did not match my needs. As a result, I had to go through much trial and error before I finally got what I really needed. They forced me to learn more about computers than I wanted to. Surely, you might say, all I had to do was ask the salesperson to take some time to explore my needs. It's not that simple. At the time, I did not even know which questions to ask. I assumed all computers could do the job I wanted. All printers are the same, aren't they? Of course not! Yet I was too ignorant to know and did not know how to ask. How I wished for a caring salesperson!

Too late now! I have learned all I need to know about computers, monitors, printers, modems, programs and all the other things that affect my business. Now I no longer need a salesperson. Now I can shop over the Internet, in catalogs and, occasionally, a computer store. One good salesperson could have saved me all this hassle and made me a customer for life.

So, understanding the needs of the farmer and how to best fulfill those needs is the first step towards a quality sale. Getting the farmer exactly what he needs for the present job while taking into account growth potential in his business is important. When a salesperson can provide this "consultative" approach to the farmer, price becomes secondary.

It won't go away. So, knowing what the competition can offer at the same or better prices is essential to helping the customer see the value of what he is getting and to appreciate the reason for a higher price, if necessary. The piece should be priced fairly. This does not mean it should be lower than the competition or even meet the price of the competition. It means that the price should be fair in relationship to the market. It should certainly be at a level that allows the dealer to make a decent profit.

If the dealer does not make a fair profit, it is not a good deal. If the farmer is not happy, it is also not a good deal. Bad deals have a habit of biting you in the butt at a later stage, sometimes way later.

Some time ago, one of my colleagues was briefing me on a workshop he had sold. He dismissed the details saying, "They paid peanuts for it, so we don't have to worry too much." We sat down immediately to discuss this. I reminded him that, if the customer paid peanuts, it was because he had done a bad selling job. Second, regardless of how much the customer paid, we were obligated to maintain our high standards and we would deliver as if he had paid top dollar.

This may seem obvious to most salespeople and sales managers. However, this was not a rookie salesperson talking. It just shows how easily we can fall into the trap of providing inferior service because we did not get the right price in the first place.

There should be a profit in every sale. That profit should be immediate and not dependent on some future, optimistic event. For example, I have heard salespeople take a trade at ridiculously high prices and justify it by saying, "Well, we'll eventually sell it. Every piece has value." They had no idea to whom they were going to sell it.

I have watched salespeople quote a profit-crunching low price and then explain it by saying, "We'll make it up on parts and service later." They had no guarantee that the customer would even come back to them for the parts and service. In one case, the customer had a history of going elsewhere for parts and service and still the salesperson used this justification.

Does it mean that you should not trade when the price on your piece is too low or the cost of the trade is too high, or both? Not necessarily. You could have other valid business reasons for making that trade. However, this becomes a business decision and not a desperation move.

I have taught many salespeople in dealerships the value of a technique I call Six Prospects. This requires the salesperson to ask himself – before he takes any trade-in – which six prospects do I know who would buy this piece, why should they buy it and how much are they likely to pay me for it? In some dealerships, this has become the standard method for evaluating trades and it has paid off big.

Now, let's get back to a quality sale. Obviously, a quality sale includes all of the above. An ideal sale would be one where the farmer's needs are met exactly, he is happy with the equipment and the price, the dealer makes an immediate and fair profit on the deal, the dealer has a home for the trade at a reasonable profit, and there are genuine prospects for selling parts and service to this farmer later.

Let me add one other piece to the ideal sale – there should be reasonable prospects of selling additional equipment to this farmer later. The good salesperson does not always take just the sale in front of him. He is always looking ahead for additional sales to the same customer. He is practicing a technique I teach called "unfolding". This means that, even as he is making one sale, he is already laying the seeds for additional sales down the road. An ideal sale is all of what I have said before plus the discovery of additional future sales.

So here is an updated definition of an ideal sale: one in which the farmer's needs are met exactly, he is happy with the equipment and the price, the dealer makes an immediate and fair profit on the deal, the dealer has a home for the trade at a reasonable profit, there are genuine prospects of selling parts and service to this farmer later, and the salesperson has uncovered future sales to this same customer.

Now, obviously, a quality sale has the same definition. However, there could be some pieces missing and the sale could still be regarded as a quality sale.

The sales manager must define what he regards as a quality sale and make sure that all salespeople in the dealership understand exactly what he means. Whenever there are deviations from his definition, the salesperson should always have to consult with his sales manager before proceeding. The sales manager should deviate very rarely from his definition. If he does, it should only be after he has thought it through properly. The definition of a quality sale then becomes part of the policies of the dealership. One deviates from policy only in exceptional circumstances.

CHAPTER 5 - ASSERTIVE MANAGEMENT

One of the first things I expect managers to do before I work with them is to take the SPQ® Call Reluctance® test. This tells me a great deal about the things a manager is likely to do that can affect his management style. One of the things I look for is how much Yielder™ Call Reluctance® he has.

Yielder™ Call Reluctance® causes sales managers to manage like wimps. Always wanting to be liked, they pander to the whims of their salespeople. They tend to be inconsistent in their directives, changing to suit the circumstances. Policies are merely guidelines. Non-negotiable behavior does not exist; everything is negotiable. They constantly defend their salespeople even in the face of overwhelming evidence that they are not performing well. They encourage "relationship building" training that forgets the reasons for the relationships. They constantly send mixed messages to their salespeople. Salespeople are quick to take advantage of a Yielder™ sales manager. They regularly get away with things that other sales managers would never tolerate. You would think that they would love a Yielder™ sales manager.

They don't. They show no respect for him and even make fun of him behind his back, sometimes to his face.

If you're getting the idea that a Yielder™ sales manager is not assertive, you're right. The biggest problem is that this sales manager thinks that the opposite of assertion is aggression. He's wrong. The opposite of assertiveness is wimpiness. Aggression is a totally different behavior. People can be assertive and aggressive but they cannot be assertive and wimpy or aggressive and wimpy.

WHAT IS ASSERTIVE SALES MANAGEMENT?

In practical terms, assertive sales management consists of doing assertive things. It means creating fair and useful policies and then enforcing them without apology. It means putting the interests of the dealership first and then taking into account the feelings and interests of others, including the salespeople. It means being proud of the dealership and expecting the same level of pride from the salespeople. It means making sure that the dealership does business fairly, profitably and consistently. And it means sending the right messages consistently.

WHY ASSERTIVE SALES MANAGEMENT?

The sales manager is an important leader in the dealership. Salespeople look to him for guidance in a variety of everyday events. Others in the dealership look to him to control and develop his salespeople. They want to know what he stands for and where they stand with him.

Customers look to the sales manager as an authority figure in the dealership and want to feel that he is interested in their problems while making sure that the dealership does not suffer. As one farmer said to me, "He should be a fair leader." Customers don't reasonably expect a sales manager to sell the dealership down the river. They simply want a fair deal and they simply want him to listen fairly to them.

Salespeople prefer an assertive sales manager. They know he has character and they know they cannot get away with silly things with him. He will not tolerate mediocrity and he will help them develop to their true potentials. They know that he has their best interests at heart but will not deviate from policy just to please them. They know that they will be treated fairly and that he has no personal agendas to destroy their careers. They trust him.

This does not mean that they will automatically like him. However, they will certainly respect him. This was something I had to learn. Before I fixed my own Yielder™ Call Reluctance®, I was that wimpy sales manager. I thought that if I could get my people to like me, the respect would automatically come. I found out that this is not the way it works. People may like you – as they did me – and still not respect you – as they did not respect me. I found that getting the respect first can cause the liking to follow. However, the opposite is not true. Liking does not automatically generate respect.

My advice to sales managers is to get the respect first. Let the liking come later and, if it does not come, so what? Respect is not automatic, either. You must earn the respect. Guess how you earn it? By being an assertive sales manager!

MY SALES MANAGER IS A WIMP!

Ron was a young, energetic salesperson in a dealership in South Dakota. Customers loved him for his vibrant energy and genuine caring for their needs. He was also popular in the dealership. So, it came as a surprise when his sales manager received a vicious complaint from a customer. The customer complained that Ron had given him the wrong price on a new tractor that was currently on a special deal. He said that Ron did not tell him that this tractor carried certain incentives.

The sales manager sympathized with the customer and told him he would handle the sale himself and make sure the customer received all the incentives due to him. In fact, he told him, he would throw in a few extras to make up for it and he would severely reprimand Ron.

Later that day, he met with Ron and explained to him that the customer preferred to deal directly with him (the sales manager) but he would pass on part of the commission to him. He felt that this was the best way to handle the situation. Ron did not question the sales manager since he was getting part of the action anyway.

Ron found out what had really happened only months later. He immediately confronted the sales manager who tried to gloss over it as if nothing had happened. Ron insisted on an explanation and this was the first time he discovered the truth. It seems there was another side to the story. He had never given the farmer a price because it had never come up. As far as he was concerned, they had not reached any agreements on the tractor because the farmer was still trying to decide which tractor to get.

"Why," he asked his sales manager, "did you not just simply tell me the truth?" "I knew you were a good person and I didn't want you to think that I believed the farmer and I didn't want to hurt your feelings." The sales manager was mortified. "Well," Ron asked, "what are you going to do about it now?" "Oh, it's water under the bridge," the sales manager said. "The farmer got away with one but don't worry, this will not happen again." Ron was confused and angry and he had every right to be.

HOW DO YOU BECOME ASSERTIVE?

I am no expert on assertion. There are many books written on assertion and I have read quite a few of them. For the most part, they helped me to understand more about assertion but they had very little practical value. It really hit me when a good friend, Don McCree, a psychologist from San Antonio, told me that for assertion training to work, it must be job-specific. That's when I started to learn assertion from the viewpoint of my own job. It made a whole lot of sense to me. Rather than deal with concepts often inappropriate to my situations, I could now deal with it on a much more basic and practical level.

Here's what I did. Perhaps this can help you too. Each day, before making calls, I would run one situation that I would face that day through my mind. I would visualize the situation as I would normally handle it. Then I would run it through my mind again, this time handling it in an assertive manner. Then I would handle that situation as soon as I could that day in an assertive manner. Most times, I liked the results from the assertive handling. There were times when I didn't but I could always find a reason why the situation did not go as expected and I could accept that reason.

I did this exercise every day for several weeks. After a while, I saw differences in the way I was handling situations that I had not visualized. I was starting to become more assertive. It also seemed as if everyone around me was noticing, too.

I'll admit that I was very skeptical at first. I was afraid that people would not like me if I acted too assertively. (My Yielder™ Call Reluctance® would not give up easily!) So, I devised some escape routes. I would practice my assertive handling of the situation I had visualized and then literally run for cover to see what would happen. At first, I could not believe what I saw. Instead of people hating me, as I expected, they actually seemed to warm up to me. Nobody tried to kill me. In fact, the opposite happened. People actually started to take me more seriously. They started to respect me for who I was and what I did. That respect has made it easier for me to sell and –

here's the nice part – it has made me a lot of money! I will be the first to admit that this is probably not the clinical way to go about acquiring assertiveness. I can imagine another friend, an unnamed behavioral scientist, wincing and throwing his hands up in despair. He knows the right way. He was trained to know the right way. I wasn't and I don't care. It worked very well for me. Perhaps it can work for you, too. I even have the nerve to teach this in one of the workshops I conduct!

SALES MANAGERS ALWAYS TEACH SALESPEOPLE

One of the important parts of assertive management is sending consistent messages. The sales manager is always teaching his salespeople and his salespeople are always learning from him. These lessons are often in the guise of innocuous messages, memos and other forms of communication. This includes the behavior of the sales manager. One of the big dangers that sales managers should avoid is being inconsistent in these lessons.

For example, a salesperson arrives late for a sales meeting. The sales manager jumps all over him and berates him in front of the group. At the next sales meeting, he arrives late again. This time the sales manager is so preoccupied with what he will say that he ignores the latecomer's entrance. He has just sent a message that it's okay to arrive late and the last time he simply had a bad-hair day.

Here's another example of sending the wrong messages. I was conducting a class for a group of salespeople and their sales manager in a dealership. We were talking about ethics. The sales manager spoke up very convincingly about being honest in your dealings with customers. He was a paragon of virtue. I had a lot of respect for him before and this elevated him in my eyes.

Later that same day, a salesperson told of a lady who had come into the dealership looking for a lawn mower. They had a particular model on sale for $200 below the normal price and this was advertised in the local papers. She had a useless lawn mower she wanted to trade in. She did not know about the sale price. The salesperson did not tell her about the $200 discount on the sale mower. Instead, he sold it to her at the list price but allowed her $200 for her trade. He wanted to know if he did the right thing. After all, he reasoned, she got what she wanted and was happy.

I asked him why he had lied. He looked dumbfounded. As far as he was concerned, he had not lied. He had simply avoided telling the truth. I pointed out very practical reasons why this was not a clever way to sell. The obvious one was that the same mower was advertised in the local paper in a small town at $200 below what she had paid. Surely he did not think her neighbors would miss it even if she did?

At that point, the sales manager jumped in and told the salesperson that he had done the right thing. It was okay, he said, to do business that way. She got what she wanted and the dealership had made its profit. He praised him for lying. However, he also contended that the salesperson had not actually lied and so that was okay. Besides, he told the group, we needed to get rid of that mower anyway.

This is an example of sending mixed messages. Earlier that day, it was a sin to lie. Now it became okay because a sale had been made. In other words, his high ethical standards were determined not by what he believed but by a sale in front of him.

I don't know how the salespeople felt about this because I terminated the class early and left. I had seen all I wanted and I knew that I did not want any more dealings with this dealership. The sales manager had dropped dramatically in my estimation.

MANAGING IRON SALESPEOPLE

In all fairness, apart from this one incident, I had never seen him do anything unethical or encourage his salespeople to do anything unethical. Also, he is a very effective sales manager who raised sales in this dealership to new highs. I am just disappointed that his ethics could not have remained intact for the duration of that one workshop.

The sales manager must always be aware of the impact he has on his salespeople.

CHAPTER 6 - TERRITORIES

One question that often arises in a dealership is whether to assign specific territories or to allow salespeople to pick up sales wherever they can in the dealer's trade area.

In the case of the smaller dealer with one salesperson, this is not a problem. In practical terms, that salesperson already has a territory. Where there are more salespeople, however, it can be a vexing problem, particularly if the dealership has operated for many years without assigned territories. That's when salespeople rebel because they feel they will lose some of their best customers. Dealerships tend to experiment with different scenarios. In my opinion, they do not let these experiments run long enough to fully determine what is best for them. They tend to give up easily.

My view is that it is always better to assign territories. Here's why: The salesperson assigned to a particular territory becomes responsible for all sales in that territory. It becomes his responsibility to ensure that all possible sales in that territory are generated and he is accountable for those sales. With proper guidance and supervision, he can fully exploit his territory. He also gets the opportunity to really learn all about the farmers in his territory and can become an expert on the farming practices there. One argument against this is that he may become complacent, taking only the easy sales and developing the habit of running the same trap lines over and over again. He may ignore opportunities because he is already doing reasonably well and his own needs are being met. However, this is the job of the sales manager. He should make sure that this does not happen, and he can take steps to prevent it from happening in the first place.

Besides, assigning territories is a more organized way of doing business. It provides very clear direction for all the salespeople. It also helps those in other departments to refer potential customers to the right salesperson. The sales manager could devise a method for rewarding a salesperson who happens to sell in someone else's territory. This could happen if a customer comes into the store while his salesperson is out. If there is no reward, there is no incentive for the salesperson in the store to do anything else except tell the customer to come back later. However, the reward should never exceed the commission that the original salesperson should receive. This can lead to poaching and disputes.

DEFINING A TERRITORY

How a territory is defined depends on the geography surrounding a dealership. There may be natural geographic boundaries or the sales manager may have to become creative. Whichever way the territories are defined, they should be clear cut and not have any fuzzy boundaries. After all, salespeople have a right to know exactly what their responsibilities are and what they are not. Whenever there can be disputes about territories, there will be.

Once territories have been defined, the sales manager should make sure that all salespeople and everyone else in the dealership understand them. It will be up to the sales manager to settle any territorial disputes later so he may as well make his job easier up front.

The territories should never be so large as to make it impossible for the salesperson to properly manage it. When this is unavoidable, it is an indication that more salespeople may be needed.

ASSIGNING TERRITORIES

When the territories are assigned to each salesperson, the sales manager should make sure that the following are understood and agreed to:

1. The geographical or other boundaries.
2. The salesperson for the territory agrees with the assignment.
3. The salesperson believes that he can effectively cover the territory.
4. The salesperson understands that he is solely responsible for the development of business in his territory.
5. All salespeople understand the compensation program if they sell outside of their assigned territories.

The sales manager could hold a special sales meeting to explain this. He should also visit with each salesperson individually to reinforce his instructions.

WORKING THE TERRITORY

The sales manager should make clear his expectations regarding how a territory should be worked and the consequences of not working it properly. There should be no doubt in the minds of his salespeople as to what those expectations or consequences are.

Working a territory means extracting every piece of available business from it that can reasonably be had. This business should be defined in terms of the sales manager's concept of what constitutes a quality sale. It should also be determined by the resources of the dealership.

Each salesperson should be taught how to work his territory. Assuming that he knows can be a vital error. Just because he has personally farmed in the area and knows just about everyone there does not mean he will know how to mine it.

The first job of a salesperson in a new territory is to plan well. He should have very clear behavioral expectations. The sales manager should help him set up a proper plan of attack. One of the first things he will need to have at his disposal is how much business he can reasonably expect from it. This requires some research.

SEGMENTING

One of the most effective methods for estimating the amount of business in the territory is segmenting. I had mentioned this earlier but it is important enough for me to repeat it.

The salesperson should divide his territory into smaller segments. He should plot all the dealer's existing customers on this smaller segment. Then, using manufacturer information, plat maps and driving, he should identify every possible prospect in that segment. He should then create a table that lists all his customers with the names of every prospect on either side of each customer.

He should gather information on every prospect. He can start with fellow employees in the dealership, asking them if they know any of the prospects.

Once he has done this for each segment, he should have a clearer idea of how much business is available and how he can best proceed to get it.

Each salesperson should be shown how to do this.

DEVELOPING A STRATEGIC SALES PLAN

Each salesperson should be shown how to develop a strategic sales plan for his territory. Then, he should develop one. A strategic sales plan means an organized plan of attack.

It includes the number of days that should be spent in the territory as opposed to time spent in the dealership, the number of people to call each week, the frequency of calls on existing customers, follow-up strategies, and so on. Activities should take into account the seasonality of the territory.

The strategic sales plan should begin with the target for the territory that the sales manager and the salesperson agree on. This target should be defined according to the amount of business available. It should also be broken down in terms of units. There should be a separate target for the number of new customers that must be acquired as well as other-color customers that should be converted. The sales manager should guide salespeople so that the targets set are realistic and achievable but not without some challenge.

MANAGING IRON SALESPEOPLE

Once the targets have been set, the salesperson should develop a plan that will include the things he will need to do to reach the targets. This plan should be in a month-by-month format.

First, he should put down the sales that are already pending plus those that seem to automatically occur each year with certain customers. While these are never givens, history has shown that these sales can reasonably be counted on to repeat in the next year. These sales should be placed in the months in which they are expected to occur.

Next, he should list all the activities that will happen, no matter what. These include open house days, special seasonal promotions, training days, vacation days, busy times when farmers are not available for buying wholegoods and any other scheduled activities. This will leave the time available for selling and the acquiring of new customers and new business.

Now he should look at the equipment targets. This will tell him when he can reasonably sell that equipment. He should list the existing customers who are likely to buy the equipment and when, and place their names in those months. He should plan to call on them in the months he has selected.

What he will have left now are the following:

1. How many additional sales dollars are required?
2. The number of pieces of equipment and the types that need to be sold.
3. How much time he has available.

This will guide him on how to spend his available time. His first priority, obviously, will be to use the time to achieve his sales targets. Proper planning will also allow him to target any other-color customers for conversion and to call on the other prospects that have been avoided or missed before.

Does this sound like hard work? You bet it is. However, this is the way professional salespeople attack a market. The salesperson in a dealership should become such a professional, and it is up to the sales manager to make sure that it happens. The sales manager should understand that, for most salespeople in dealerships, this is not an easy task and that they will find excuses to avoid this type of detailed planning. Many may not even know how to begin. This is where the sales manager comes in. He should coach them on how to do it. Note that I said coach them and not do it for them. This type of coaching can have long-lasting effects for the dealership and for each salesperson. While the salespeople will kick and scream, they will eventually thank the sales manager who forces them to do it.

This plan need not have the smaller details. Rather, it should be a guide that is updated weekly. Each week, the salesperson should develop a weekly plan that corresponds to the master plan. This weekly plan should then be updated daily. The sales manager should examine these plans and help whenever needed.

CALL FREQUENCIES

How often should a salesperson call on each customer? This depends on the customer. Very good customers require more call frequencies. If they are big spenders, and most good customers are, they are vulnerable to attack from the competition. The dealership should protect these customers as much as possible. One way to protect them is to provide such good service that the customer has no need to go elsewhere.

Salespeople in dealerships often tell me that customers don't want to be contacted every month. I disagree. I think that

MANAGING IRON SALESPEOPLE

NOBODY INVADES MY TERRITORY!

Randy felt that he worked his territory as best he could and he was giving the dealership respectable numbers. His sales manager knew that he was also leaving behind many sales. He had calculated how much the territory was worth in terms of new business and Randy was only producing about half that amount. He figured, correctly, that an additional salesperson was needed to properly work the territory.

Randy went ballistic when he suggested this!

"I have worked my butt off in this territory!" he yelled. "You're not putting anyone else in there and that's that."

The sales manager had expected this outburst. He had always been defensive about his territory. So, he shelved the idea one more time. Then I came on the scene. I traveled with Randy one day. At the end of the day, he gave me a smug look.

"Did you learn anything?" he asked.

"Yes," I replied. "I learned that you're not as hot as you think you are." We had bonded during the day as two good salespeople usually do. This was why I was allowed to be so cocky.

"What makes you say that?" he asked. He knew I meant no offence.

I told him about the opportunities he had driven by and the huge expanse of his territory. I told him that, by his own admission, he could never cover his territory as effectively as he would like to.

"What you need is some help, someone who can handle some of the smaller stuff so that you can be free to take care of the bigger deals."

"You know, my sales manager has been trying to get me to do that," he said. "but I think he's just trying to get me out."

"You know you're more valuable than that. Why don't you suggest that he brings a new salesperson in and allows you to train him the way you do business. If you're clever, you can even ask for a piece of his commission while he is under your wing."

"You're not so bad after all," he smiled. "Spend another day with me and you might show me how to take over the dealership."

"You would hate that," I told him.

A week later, they hired another salesperson and Randy took great delight in introducing him to his customers as his "sidekick".

customers would be happy to be contacted every day if there was a good enough reason – from the customer's point of view – for this contact. The best customers should be contacted each month. The salesperson should find good valid business reasons for these contacts. The contacts could be via telephone, fax or even email. However, one face-to-face meeting each month is not unreasonable.

The number of contacts per customer should depend on one thing only – is there a good valid business reason for the contact from the customer's perspective? Therefore, salespeople should develop an inventory of valid business reasons for contacting their best customers.

Certain contacts have to be made. These include selling appointments, follow-up meetings, planning meetings and delivery appointments. The last one has gotten me more arguments from salespeople than almost anything else I have taught them.

I will maintain until the day I die that the salesperson should be present when the customer takes delivery of a new piece of equipment or even a used piece. Farm equipment is not cheap. It usually involves a substantial investment on the part of the farmer. It certainly costs more than a car. Yet, salespeople habitually avoid being there when he takes delivery. Instead, they send it out with the set-up technician. They claim that they do not have the time. My answer is simple – make the time. If a car salesperson can make the time to be present when a customer takes delivery of a new or used car, surely the farm equipment salesperson can at least do the same. Think about it. How would you like it if the auto dealership delivered your new car to your home with a mechanic?

The other reason given is that it takes so much planning. You have to get the set-up guy there plus you have to make sure that the farmer is there. I have asked salespeople, "Are you planning a military attack?" Coordinating the schedules of two or more people is not rocket science.

Perhaps one of the set-up technicians I spoke to provides the true answer. The reason why salespeople avoid these calls, he said, is because they do not know how to walk the customer around the machine. What an indictment on the salesperson! The sales manager should make sure that his salespeople know how to deliver a machine and then insist that they do.

Other contacts that have to be made include first contacts with new prospects and then follow-up contacts with them. These include the other-color farmers. One of the complaints I often hear from dealer owners is that their salespeople do not follow up properly or consistently on inquiries they receive or on quotes they have given. The sales manager should devise a proper follow up procedure that all salespeople must adhere to.

SALES MANAGER EXPECTATIONS

One of the best things a sales manager can do for salespeople is to provide very clear expectations. Earlier I said that salespeople would like to please their sales manager but often do not know what he wants. Many times, when a salesperson does not please the sales manager, it is the fault of the sales manager. He had not made his expectations clear. The sales manager should make sure all new and veteran salespeople know exactly what is required of them. If he does this when a new salesperson starts, it prevents problems down the road. When it comes to veterans, he should develop his expectations and then communicate them clearly to all the existing salespeople. He should explain why he wants them to meet those expectations and lay out clear consequences if they do not.

What expectations should be made clear? Here is a list:

1. *Professional Appearance.* This includes dress, neatness, cleanliness of company vehicles and anything else that impacts on the way the salesperson appears to the customer.
2. *Procedures.* These include complete paperwork and the adherence to follow-up and other procedures. These procedures should be clarified and explained.
3. *Targets.* These include volume targets, equipment targets, new customer targets and other-color conversion targets.
4. *Activities.* These include the number of calls, including phone calls, per day, planning, reports, country visits, in-store hours, attending sales meetings, and any other dealership activities that the salesperson is expected to perform.
5. *Education.* This lays out the minimum knowledge requirements and the time that should be devoted each week to increasing this knowledge.
6. *Territory.* This defines what the salesperson is expected to do to properly work and manage his territory.

These expectations should be in written form and handed to each salesperson.

THE ROLE OF THE CSR

The Customer Service Representative can help the salesperson develop a territory. However, the responsibility is still with the salesperson. He should never be allowed to deflect this responsibility to the CSR. I have seen too many examples of dealer salespeople deflecting responsibilities for their jobs to the hapless CSR who eventually becomes bogged down with salesperson activities. While the CSR can help in the collection of profiles, for example, this is still the responsibility of the salesperson. The CSR should help to update the machinery portion of the profile but the salesperson should be the one to initiate it and to gather the business information.

Salespeople should meet regularly with the CSR to discuss what he has observed on their territories. Particular attention should be paid to new business opportunities. The salesperson should also report to the CSR any parts and service business opportunities that he has come across. The CSR is a valuable member of the dealership team. He is the eyes and ears of the entire dealership. He is constantly calling on farmers, talking to them and observing them in action. He is likely to be one of the first to know about the future plans of a customer, equipment that is ready to fail or special needs of certain farmers. He can also gauge the mood of farmers. These are all valuable data for the salesperson who can use it to further his own understanding of his customers.

The CSR should be briefed by the sales department on the things they would like him to observe and report on. For example, when a farmer is spending a lot of time repairing an older piece of equipment, the salesperson should know so that he can talk to him about replacing it. If the CSR notices the competitor salesperson talking to one of the customers of the dealership, this should be reported at once.

The sales manager should not assume that the CSR already knows what to look for. He should get his sales team together and create a list of things that they want the CSR to look for. There should be a proper system for reporting this. Perhaps the CSR needs a reporting form.

Once a week, the salespeople should meet with the CSR. They should have a list of questions to ask him. This will help them keep their fingers on the pulse of their territories.

CHAPTER 7 - CUSTOMER SATISFACTION

Much has been made of customer satisfaction in dealerships long before it became popular in other industries. Even so, there is some misunderstanding about what it means in practical terms.

Manufacturers have done a great job of drumming customer satisfaction into the heads of dealers. They have always known that, in order to maintain or grow market share, you must have satisfied customers. And so they rate their dealers on the CSI - customer satisfaction index.

THE CSI

What is the CSI? This is an overall rating of a dealership from a recent customer's perspective. After a piece of equipment has been sold, the manufacturer sends out a questionnaire to the customer, who completes and returns it. Often, these returned questionnaires are shared with the dealer, especially when the customer has written some bad comments. This is when the company's representative will have a "serious" meeting with the dealer and find ways to correct any complaints.

Mostly, the CSI is kept as a measuring stick. Dealers are rated according to the overall percentage points they receive. One of the biggest values of the CSI is that it gives the customer an opportunity to voice grievances and the dealer an opportunity to respond. One of the inherent flaws of such a system is that it depends on volume responses to be an accurate gauge. At an individual level, one has to distrust at least some of the information. There are some people, for example, who will rate a dealer highly regardless of how they really feel. They don't want to offend anyone. Then there are those who regularly rate dealers low even when they are completely satisfied. For them, a six on a ten-point scale is high. I have seen dealers groan in agony when they see these returns.

Still, the CSI has validity and the dealer should take it seriously. I would be more concerned with customer loyalty than customer satisfaction.

CUSTOMER LOYALTY

When a customer keeps coming back to you despite the fact that he has other options, then you are doing something right regardless of the CSI index. However, in today's volatile market, one cannot take customer loyalty for granted. There are different degrees of customer loyalty.

Not long ago, I heard a manufacturer's regional managers talking about how loyal their customers were to their color. I heard a great deal about color loyalty. Funny, I have not been hearing too much about this lately. Perhaps manufacturers are starting to realize that there is no longer that color loyalty that they thought there was. There may be a color preference and, in fact, there is ample evidence that there is. But color loyalty? Offer a green farmer a red tractor for $1 and see how long that loyalty lasts.

CHANGING COLOR

I had heard too many times that customers are so loyal to one color that they will not change. Salespeople in dealerships had told me too many times about how useless it was to call on competitive owners. I never believed any of this. So, I decided to ask the customer.

I chose farmers at random. The only qualifying criterion was that they should be predominantly one color. It didn't matter to me what color they were as long as that color dominated. I went to see twelve such farmers at the end of 1999. I asked all of them the same question, "What would it take for you to change color just once?"

The first response I always got was that this was not going to happen. Then they realized I was not selling them anything and they opened up to me. (It tickled me that they thought I was there to sell them farm equipment. Anyone who knows me, knows that I don't look at all like an equipment salesperson!)

What they told me was eye opening. First, price was never even mentioned. They told me what it would take to get them to consider changing color and these applied no matter what color they had. Their conditions are summarized below.

1. Patience — to switch may be a tough emotional decision.
2. Persistence — keep calling even when it looks like there is no hope.
3. Integrity — don't discuss my business with others.
4. Tact — don't contact my dealer or let him know I'm considering a switch.
5. Respect — don't belittle the product I already have.

MANAGING IRON SALESPEOPLE

I believe there are many customers who prefer a certain color and would like to remain with that color forever. Economic conditions, changes in dealerships and other factors put a dent in this, however. I believe there are many customers who are loyal to their dealership more than they are to the color. They have developed a dependence on a dealership they feel comfortable with. Usually, but not always, the dealership has done enough to have earned that loyalty.

Even then, this loyalty is fragile. It depends on too many factors. A change in the ownership of the dealership or the farm can affect this loyalty. An aggressive marketing campaign from a neighboring dealership can at least upset it. One poor customer service contact can weaken it.

Fragile as this loyalty can be, the dealership has to make every effort to cultivate loyal customers. This means that everyone in the dealership should be aware of the customer loyalty policy of the dealership and everyone in the dealership should be concerned with customer loyalty. More, they should be doing things to nail down this loyalty. The salesperson plays a pivotal role. Many times, the other employees observe how the salesperson treats the customer, both when the customer is in and when he has left. They take their cues from the salesperson. Salespeople should set an example for the rest of the dealership when it comes to treating customers right. The sales manager should make sure this happens and should never allow even one small slip to go unchallenged.

There are things the sales manager can do to foster this customer loyalty.

1. Make sure that the salespeople really know their customers. This does not mean knowing what they bought last year. It means an in-depth knowledge of their businesses, what their plans are and who they are. The proper use of profiles will

help. This should be an important part of the duties of salespeople.
2. Develop a proper follow-up and follow-through system. Nothing should be allowed to fall through the cracks.

PROFILES - KNOWING THE CUSTOMER

Profiles are a hotly debated issue in dealerships and often a thorny subject. Many salespeople hate the profile. Most salespeople do not know what a true profile is or what it can do for them. Many see it as a nuisance, something the manufacturer wants them to do that has no value. They complain about the time it takes and the fact that their customers are not willing to share the information with them. They claim that the customer sees this as an intrusion into their privacy. Whenever they first see the Sales Academy Profile Form, they roll their eyes and groan. Their first reaction is that there is no way that they will get the customer to give them all of the information.

Before we look at the profile itself, we should agree on some things.

1. It is the duty of the salesperson to gather enough information on his customers to be able to serve them effectively and efficiently. The salesperson *should* know about the customer and the business of the customer. Any salesperson in a dealership who disagrees with this may already be beyond salvation.
2. If you do not know enough about the business of your customer, you cannot develop him into one of those loyal customers we discussed earlier.
3. If you do not have the right information on your best cus-

tomers, they are vulnerable to poaching from the competition.
4. Time spent learning the business of your customer is the best learning time you can spend.
5. Having the information in your head, as claimed by some salespeople, is not acceptable.
6. Most of the information on a profile of a good customer should already be available somewhere in the dealership.

The profile is an ideal method for collecting and then analyzing this data.

WHY SALESPEOPLE HATE PROFILES

Some years back, a few manufacturers saw the value of profiles and passed this information to their dealers. Some dealers got their salespeople to begin collecting profiles. Back then, however, a profile consisted of some rudimentary information about the customer and a list of his equipment. This information was stored somewhere in the dealership's files and nothing much was done with it. Soon salespeople stopped collecting them.

Next, the manufacturers pointed out the value of collecting equipment information. If the farmer's wife came in for a part and you had the serial numbers of his equipment, they said, it became easier to find the right part for her. There were also some service benefits. This got dealers to start again on the profiles. This effort did not last long. Salespeople wised up to this in a hurry. "Why should we collect these profiles?" they asked, "If the parts and service departments need this information, let them get it. It's hard work, you know."

Not to be outdone, the manufacturers came back with

another good reason for collecting profiles. Whenever you need a certain piece of used equipment for one of your customers, they said, you could do a cross search of your database and locate the farmers who had that type of equipment. Also, promotions become easier since you can do a search for all your customers who have the equipment you want to base your promotion on. This allows you to target them more precisely. This made a great deal of sense to dealers who now urged their salespeople to get out there and get those profiles.

The effort has always been half-hearted, though. Even when they did a thorough job, the data magically disappeared into computers and were not used often enough to warrant the effort. Then the data became outdated because nobody was updating the profiles. In one case, I came across a profile of a customer who had 15 combines. "Obviously a mistake," the salesperson told me.

This is not to say that there are no dealers who make better use of the profiles. There are but they are rare. I once read the report on a customer focus meeting in which the customers of a certain dealership were discussing a salesperson from a competing dealership. "It seems," they said, "that he always knows what we want, when we want it, and even before we know it. If we trade every year, he knows it and he is there at the right time. He always has a good reason for calling on us." I'll bet my boots that this salesperson uses profiles wisely.

HOW TO USE A PROFILE

First, I agree with the salesperson who says it is a waste of time collecting profiles. If I were the salesperson, I would not waste my time doing something that has no benefit for me. The

MANAGING IRON SALESPEOPLE

profiles I have seen would have wasted my time.

This is why a newer, better profile is needed. Sales Academy created one and makes it available to dealers. It also teaches dealer salespeople how to use it. This profile contains relevant information about the farmer, his business and his plans for the future. It looks at purchasing habits for wholegoods, parts and service. It intelligently estimates total purchases and compares this to what the dealer is currently getting. It identifies the gap between the two and allows the salesperson to develop a target for closing this gap.

My idea of a profile is that it should help me get more business. If it cannot do that, I would not be too keen to use it. Properly done, a profile helps the salesperson to look into the future with the customer and to identify future business, sometimes even before the customer does.

Mark Nelson, a savvy John Deere dealer in South Dakota once told me, "In the next 12 months, every one of the farmers in my trade area will trade at least one piece of equipment. The trick is to know who and when."

Actually, he had already answered one of the questions. Who? He had said every one of the farmers in his trade area. If he was right, then every farmer became a candidate. When? That's where the profile comes in. Properly collected and analyzed, it will tell you not only when but also which pieces. This is powerful information. Let's say the profile indicates the farmer is likely to change a certain piece in October. It does not help much to call on that farmer in October. By then, everyone else will know. Perhaps the best time would be to call and discuss the trade in September or even August. This makes you look like a genius. Also, you may be able to close the deal before your competitors even get to hear about it.

To be able to do this, the profile must contain enough business information besides the equipment inventory of the farmer. The salesperson must have had an in-depth discussion with the farmer about his plans for the future. This information must be recorded in such a way that the salesperson is able to analyze this information and to reach logical future business conclusions.

I believe that asking salespeople to collect profiles for the sake of collecting them is counter-productive. I would rather have my salespeople collect one good, useful profile each month on my best customers and update that profile every six months than for them to collect a hundred and have these rot in my computer.

I asked salespeople in a dealership to do this once. They, like most dealer salespeople, immediately came up with objections. Before examining the profile form, they objected to its length. Then they examined some of the business questions and told me that their customers would never give out this type of information. I pointed out two major problems I had with their responses.

First, we were talking about their best customers. They had identified these as being among the top twenty customers in their dealership. If they did not have most of the information required on the form, they were already in serious trouble. If I were a competitor, I would find it easy to sneak this customer away from them.

Second, if they are as good as they claim, then they should already have developed a good business relationship with this customer, enough to be able to discuss long-term business issues. If they did not have this type of relationship, the customer is at risk of being poached and they were fooling themselves about the relationship.

The profile should contain enough business information to allow the parts and service departments to analyze it for their own purposes. Perhaps they can create parts or service programs that can lock the customer into the dealership for at least a year at a time.

Profiles should be carefully guarded. This is vital information. However, every employee should have access to it so that any employee can update it at any time.

DEVELOPING A FOLLOW THROUGH PROCESS

The sales manager can further advance the efforts to create loyal customers by developing a follow through process. There are two situations where this is needed.

Customer inquiries should be properly recorded and followed through on. The sales manager should develop a simple process that allows all inquiries to be recorded and tracked. All salespeople can carry a simple inquiry sheet. When they are in the dealership, it can be on their desks. When out, they should have them in the pickup. The Inquiry sheet looks like this -

Date	Customer	Nature	What I Promised	When?	Done

The inquiry form should be updated each day by the salesperson and a copy turned in to the sales manager at the end of each week. The sales manager should follow up with the salesperson to make sure nothing is falling through the cracks.

There should also be a process for following up after a sale has been concluded. A follow up form can be created that records the actions to be taken after the sale, the dates when these should be performed and a check that the actions were done. Each salesperson should have one form for each sale. The activities can be automated on their computers with a reminder popping up a day before the action is due.

An example of this form is shown on the next page. Of course, dealers will develop a form best suited to their customers.

The sales manager should make sure that each salesperson religiously follows this process. If there are any problems with the salesperson not doing it, the sales manager should resolve them as they come up and not wait until the process has lost its value.

If the sales manager insists on the salespeople doing the right things — learning about the business of their customers and following through on customer service — then loyal customers become easier to get and maintain.

MANAGING IRON SALESPEOPLE

Customer:	Equipment:	
Date	Action	Done
5/31/00	Equipment Sold	
6/1/00	Thank You note sent	
6/1/00	Confirmation letter sent	
6/9/00	Equipment Delivered - be there	
6/9/00	Ask for referral	
6/16/00	Check with customer on satisfactory use	
7/21/00	Call customer - satisfaction survey	
8/11/00	Call customer on service	
9/8/00	Call customer about options	
4/6/01	Warranty issues	
4/26/01	Call customer - trade?	

CHAPTER 8 - COMPETITION

"If I were your competitor," I have often told dealers. "I would not be too concerned about your smaller customers. I would go after your best customers because I know that getting just one of them each year from you will feed my family for a long time. Losing one of them each year to me will seriously cripple your business too. If I were your competitor, I would not be overly-concerned about your well-being."

While salespeople in dealerships regularly complain about competitors — especially in-line competitors — they don't do enough to beat them. As far as they are concerned, the other dealer got the deal because he cut the price and nothing else. How silly is this?

Once I asked a dealer about a competitor down the road. His response was, "He cuts prices and makes all deals unprofitable. It's his fault that we are in the situation we're in." I then went to that dealer and asked him about his competitor up the road. Guess what he told me? "He cuts prices." It's easy for dealers to fall into this trap. Their salespeople learn very quickly what a wonderful excuse this is for not getting deals at a profit. Who do they learn this from? Perhaps the dealership needs to adopt a no-excuse policy. Or, perhaps they can get the salespeople to understand competitors better and be able to handle them.

WHAT SHOULD THE SALESPERSON LEARN ABOUT THE COMPETITION?

As much as possible! My philosophy is — you can whip them if you know them. And the more you know about your competition, the less you need to know.

Here are some things a salesperson should know.

1. The strengths and weaknesses of the competitor's sales force.
2. The capacity of the competitor to carry parts and to service equipment.
3. The reputation of the competitor in terms of sales, parts and service.
4. Their pricing policy.
5. Their trade-in policy.
6. What resources do they have from their manufacturer?
7. What financing options do they have?
8. What is the make-up of their best customers?
9. Which customers do they treat as not being part of their core business?
10. How easy is it for a customer to do business with them?
11. How stretched out is their sales force?
12. Which areas are they neglecting?
13. What short lines do they carry that you do not?
14. What short lines do they not carry that they probably should?

15. If you could sum up their biggest strength in one sentence, what would that be?
16. If you could sum up their biggest weakness in one sentence, what would that be?
17. How do you compare to them in terms of all the above?

HOW CAN A SALESPERSON FIND OUT?

One thing is certain, the information will not come through osmosis. The salesperson is going to have to act to get it. The following is an amended extract from my book, *"P.A.S.S. C.A.L.F. - 8 Behaviors of Sales Success in an Agricultural Dealership".*

HOW DO YOU LEARN ABOUT YOUR COMPETITION?

There are several ways you can learn about your competition.

1. One of the easiest is to use the resources provided by your manufacturer. They have all kinds of videos, literature, sales manuals and audiotapes available.
2. Pick up literature on competitor models and study them. Compare what they say about their equipment with what you know about yours. How is yours better? Which features can you make a strong case for? If you were a buyer, why would you buy it?
3. Ask your customers. Ask those who have purchased from your competitors. Ask them why they purchased, what benefits they got and if they are happy with their purchase. Ask those who did not purchase from the competition. Ask them why they did not. If what they tell you can help you in

another sale, ask them if you can quote them.
4. Ask your competitors' customers. Ask them why they purchased. Ask what the biggest selling point was that got them to commit. Ask, "If you had to do it all over again, would you still purchase this? Why?" Tell them about some features your product has and ask them to help you compare.
5. Read your trade magazines. Read about your competitors. Study their ads. What do you like about them? What do you not like? Track their inventory through the ads. Are the same pieces showing up or are they bringing in more than you are? Read about other equipment. Make sure you know enough about them to be able to talk about them. If there is something you don't understand, ask your colleagues or sales manager.
6. Drive onto your competitors' lots. Look around. Do they have a lot of astronaut equipment? (This is equipment taken in a trade that should never have happened at the price they paid and that now take up space.) Do they have good equipment? Come back each month and see how much of their equipment is moving and how much is staying behind. If you know your business well, you should be able to tell a great deal about your competition just by driving onto their lots once a month.
7. Discuss with your colleagues and sales manager. Teach them as well as learn from them. Don't ignore the technician who may have worked on other-color equipment. Talk to the parts person who sells parts to competitive owners. The amounts and types of parts being sold can teach you something.

As you can see, you have many resources available to you. You should use these resources to improve your knowledge of your competition. Incidentally, it drives your competition crazy when their customers come to you for advice on their equipment because it shows you know more about it than they do.

The sales manager should help the salespeople by assembling the data on competitors in an easily accessible filing system.

COMPETITION PHILOSOPHY

The sales manager should also develop a competition philosophy. There are certain deals that he will not give up, even if it means losing money. These should be very few in number, but the salespeople should know what these circumstances are.

He should make it clear to the salespeople at what point he may consider losing a deal to the competition rather than losing money. The competition policy should always let the salespeople know, in no uncertain terms, how determined the sales manager will be in the face of competition.

The sales manager should make it absolutely clear to the salespeople that he is not afraid of competition and may even welcome it in some circumstances.

Finally, the sales manager should show the salespeople how to respond to competition. Most salespeople in dealerships are afraid of competition and often respond negatively. Many times, as soon as they hear they have competition, they drop the price. A good sales manager teaches his salespeople how to resist competition without giving up the dealership. He will show them how to compare themselves to the competition and how to proudly stand up for their dealership.

WORKING WITH THE COMPETITION

In many small towns where there are two or more competing dealerships, the relationship between the dealers can become too chummy or too bitter. While it is always better to get along, one should not do so at the expense of the dealership. In some cases, the dealership may not carry a certain item because of a number of business reasons but one of the competitors does. It makes sense to work with the competitor in such a case. However, this does not mean sending your customers to the competition. Perhaps you can work out a friendly arrangement whereby you can purchase this one item at a reasonable price for resale to your customer. You can always extend an offer to do the same on items he may not stock.

One reason for business is to strengthen the community where the business is located. Ruthlessly forcing a competitor out may not be in the best interests of the community or even the dealership. Many times, having a competitor helps you. It forces you to become a better businessperson and your competitor brings customers into the area.

Bill Fogarty is someone who has been around the agricultural equipment industry longer than most and continues to write for Farm Equipment Magazine. He points out that there are times when competing dealers should work together. This typically includes farm safety promotional efforts, local chamber of commerce projects or a group auction of used equipment. In some towns, the dealers pool their resources to run a group classified ad, each dealer having space to tout his used wares. Together, they develop a bigger ad that gets more attention. The dealers who have done this have told him they think there is more net traffic drawn to the town to see the used equipment.

I believe that there can be a cordial relationship built on

mutual respect. If you show this respect first, you should reasonably expect it in return.

INTEGRITY

As part of the competition policy, the sales manager should insist that the salespeople behave with the utmost integrity at all times. This means they are not allowed to badmouth the competition at any time, no matter what the circumstances. Neither are they allowed to air their grievances about the competition to their customers or prospects. Of course, lying about the competition cannot be tolerated.

This is basic honesty and integrity that one hopes the sales manager will instill in his salespeople anyway. It just bears repeating. There are many ways to beat the competition without resorting to dishonest methods.

YOU CAN ALSO GO TOO FAR!

In one dealership, two technicians had quit and set up their own "shade tree" operation. Not only were they now competing with the dealership, they were stealing customers by cutting prices. As if this was not bad enough, they were buying their parts from the dealership.

That's not all! The parts person, who just happened to be related to one of them, was giving them special discounts on their parts and was feeding them information about the dealer's customers!

He worked the late shift and that's when they came in for their parts. Others in the dealership noticed that these two renegades even came behind the parts counter and served themselves.

Wow! That's really working with your competition!

CHAPTER 9 - WHY SALESPEOPLE FAIL

Whenever I talk about salespeople failing, I don't mean that they become totally useless and end up in homeless shelters. To me, failure is when a salesperson does not reach his or her true potential and could have. These "failures" cost companies a great deal of money and management time. Many such salespeople could have been helped if only their sales managers had shown more interest in understanding them.

What this means is that there are a lot of salespeople who already make a decent living at sales but whom I would consider failures because they are capable of doing much more. Why do salespeople fail? After all, selling is a simple process that is being successfully performed every single day by literally millions of people around the world. If it were that difficult, very little would get sold.

Is it perhaps because those who fail are stupid? Actually, according to my own definition of selling, it would not matter if they were. If it took genius to sell, we would all be in terrible trouble. In any case, most salespeople are not stupid.

Are they lazy? Don't they want to succeed? Are they afraid of success? What about lack of selling skills? That's the only thing that makes any sense. If you don't know what to do, how could you do it? However, any salesperson who has been selling for a year or longer already knows how to sell. Their selling skills may need to be honed but they do know what to do.

Mediocre sales performance can usually be traced to one or more of the following:

1. *Skill deficiency* - some salespeople genuinely don't know how to sell. They try but they don't even know when they are doing something wrong. Then there are those who know how to sell in principle but miss out on the practical experience. The sales manager can help by observing, identifying the missing skills and coaching or training the salesperson to improve the skill level. Sometimes, off-the-shelf sales training classes will help. More often, a customized approach that addresses the deficient skills in real-life situations is preferable.

2. *Fear about selling or Call Reluctance®*. Salespeople fail in huge numbers because of Call Reluctance®. Call Reluctance© causes salespeople to avoid selling situations in favor of more comfortable activities. Initiating first contact with new prospects becomes distressful and so they find other legitimate activities to occupy their time. This strikes even veteran salespeople. One of the biggest difficulties with Call Reluctance® is that the salesperson is often not even aware of it. He knows something is wrong but doesn't know what it is. He blames himself and tries to talk himself out of it, which only makes it worse. In the end, he learns to cope with it and resigns himself to living with it. It's almost as if he is abandoning his ambitions.

I will deal with Call reluctance® in detail in the next chapter. For now, the sales manager should know that he could help the salesperson overcome it.

3. *Lack of successful behaviors*. Many salespeople fail be-

cause they simply do not do enough of the right activities to generate enough prospects or new business. Those who are moderately successful habitually run the same trap lines. They call on the easy accounts, take the easy sales and give a good impression of "doing their best" in a hostile market. I have seen more of this in dealerships than in any other business where I have worked. Dealer salespeople will admit to knowing what to do and claim that they should be doing these things but they conveniently forget the very next day. Perhaps their sales managers should hold them accountable for these behaviors. However, before they can be held accountable, someone has to show them what these successful behaviors are and how to do them. I'm not talking rocket science here. I'm talking about very simple behaviors that, done consistently, almost guarantees sales success, even in a dummy. Behaviors include planning, cold calls and other consistent activities. The sales manager can help by insisting on the salespeople performing these behaviors until they become habits.

4. Lack of clear expectations. The salespeople often do not know what is expected of them. When asked what they expect of their salespeople, most managers simply say, "sell" as if that's the magic word. Of course, they should sell but can the sales manager perhaps make the expectation clearer? For example, can the sales manager tell the salesperson that he is expected to sell x number of tractors in a month or to call on x number of new customers in a week?

Many times, the reason why salespeople don't please the sales manager is because they don't know what he wants. The best sales managers let their people know very clearly what is expected of them. Salespeople appreciate this and deliver for them.

MANAGING IRON SALESPEOPLE

If you look at the above reasons for mediocre sales performance, you will see that all can be traced back to the sales manager. If, for example, the salesperson lacks training, then the sales manager should have provided the training. If the salesperson has Call Reluctance®, the sales manager should have found ways to overcome it. If the salesperson did not perform the right successful behaviors, the sales manager should have insisted and held the salesperson accountable. Of course, if the expectations of the sales manager had not been made clear, then the salesperson cannot be blamed for not meeting those expectations.

SACRED COWS AND OTHER HOLY SALESPEOPLE

On the other hand, sales managers have to deal with the sacred cows in a dealership. These are the hot-dog salespeople who consistently refuse to be managed. They buck authority and defy the sales manager to tell them what to do. They feel they know more about selling than their sales manager and cannot see the reasons for the unnecessary rules. They are doing very nicely, thank you. They don't need some weasel looking over their shoulders.

In all cases, the salesperson produces just enough business to make it difficult for the sales manager to just simply fire him. Fearful that he will leave, the sales manager manages by exception - rules apply to everyone except Jesse. He's somehow different and exempt. This salesperson terrifies the sales manager. If he makes him mad enough, he may just quit and take a whole chunk of business with him.

In some cases, this ego may even have been earned. The salesperson has done the right things consistently enough to have built a loyal following and may genuinely not need the type of management the others require. This is rare, however. In most of the cases I have observed, this ego is not justified by performance. It has never been earned.

Tom was such a case. Young, good-looking and articulate, Tom regularly sold around $4 million each year. When I first met him, he was a bit condescending. After all, what was I going to teach him? He showed me around the dealership. Standing in the shop, he pointed to the technicians hard at work.

"See those people?" he stated proudly. "They're there because of me. Look around the dealership. It is here because of me and the sales I make."

"Wow!" I was impressed. "They ought to build a statue of you outside the dealership."

"Damned right, they should," he acknowledged.

A few months later, the owner called me. Tom wanted to leave and he wanted to know what to do. I asked why Tom wanted to leave. It seems he wanted more compensation than everyone else. The dealer gave in and paid him more.

A few months later, I got another frantic call. This time, Tom wanted a better pickup or he was going to leave. He got it.

About a month after he got his better pickup, Tom left anyway and went into a completely different profession. The owner called me to tell me the good news and the bad news. The bad news was that Tom had finally left. The good news was that he had not lost one cent in business. In fact, he had gained because customers came in who had refused to come while Tom was there.

Sure, Tom was a good salesperson. Sure, he sold a lot. However, what he forgot was that customers were not buying Tom. They were buying the dealership and what that dealership, including Tom, could do for their businesses.

I have no difficulty treating a sales superstar differently if he has earned the right. I have a lot of difficulty doing it when the ego is not earned. I have very little patience with sacred cows who refuse to uphold their end of the deal. They destroy team spirit and demoralize everyone else in the dealership. The sales manager should evaluate the total effect of the behaviors of the sacred cow. In most cases, the sales manager would do well to simply slaughter him and replace him with two other salespeople, if necessary.

I remember seeing the title of a book that had nothing to do with what I'm talking about here except that the title applies - *Sacred Cows Make the Best Hamburgers.*

So, That's What You Expect From Me!

I will never forget my first selling job. It was with a company called The Assicurazione Generale of Trieste, Italy, otherwise known as Standard General Insurance Company. A sales manager had convinced me that I was perfect salesman material and that I would make a fortune selling life insurance. I'll never forget how he sat in my living room one night, painting a vision for me that really got me excited. He made all kinds of assurances. The pay was good and guaranteed (Liar!), the company would spend a great deal of time and money training me (another lie!), and I would be treated like a king wherever I went. His eyes almost closed as he described my new fortunes. I was sold!

The next day I showed up at their offices in Port Elizabeth, South Africa, ready and eager to start my new life. He introduced me to the branch manager, a red-faced, very tall, stooping, elderly man who called himself "Big Bill, the Basher" and who seemed to brighten the room with his big smile.

After the formalities, Big Bill took me to a communal office, showed me my desk, handed me a rate book and told me, "Go get 'em, kid!" I can still see that office, bleak and empty except for me sitting there, thinking, "Go get what?" I read the rate book, not understanding what I was looking at. I wondered what I was going to do. I sat there for two days, reading and wondering.

Finally, Joe, the sales manager came to see me and said

he would help. He told me to make an appointment and he would come along to show me how it was done. I looked at him.
"What's an appointment?" I asked.
He seemed mildly shocked. "You don't know what an appointment is?" "No."
"You've got friends, haven't you?" "Yes."
"So call up one of them and we'll go together."
" What will I tell them about why we want to come?"
"We're gonna sell them life insurance, of course."
"Why would they want to buy?"
"Everyone buys life insurance. Let's try something else. Which of your friends are recently married or have just had a baby?"

My face lit up. Doug and Elaine had gotten married a few months ago and had told me that Elaine had just gotten pregnant. I told Joe. His face lit up.

"Make the appointment with them," he beamed.

I did. Doug and Elaine lived on a smallholding outside of town. Joe and I called one evening. We sat in their small living room. Doug and Elaine sat on a sofa. I sat to the right of them and Joe sat opposite them. Finally, I thought, I'm going to learn how to sell life insurance.

We didn't sell anything that night. Joe started out well enough but soon appeared distracted and seemed to forget what to say. He stumbled often. I didn't learn anything about selling that night and left the meeting even more confused. I was really mad when he told me the reason he had been so distracted. Apparently, from where he was sitting, he could see up Elaine's dress! This was enough to turn him into a bumbling fool.

Looking back on it now, it was hilarious but I went home that night seething. I didn't introduce him to any more of my friends. I eventually left Standard General, joined Manufacturer's Life where I finally learned about selling and became one of their top salespeople. A year later, I started my own brokerage business and sold more life insurance policies than anyone in town. It was a rocky start that could have been made easier if I had had a professional sales manager. Still, I look back on that year with The Assicurazione Generale of Trieste, Italy, as a necessary learning experience.

CHAPTER 10 - SALES CALL RELUCTANCE®

When someone is afraid of something or is uncomfortable doing it, the natural response is to avoid doing it. Many sales managers and salespeople misunderstand Call Reluctance®. Rather than explain it, I'm going to explain an exercise I do in speeches and workshops.

Imagine a group of dealer salespeople sitting in a room.

I start the exercise by asking them if they cared about their dealership. The response is usually that they do. I then ask if they cared about their sales careers. Of course, they reply.

I tell them that I saw a story in the local paper that morning about someone I thought could be a prospect for a new tractor. He was happy with the dealer that he was with, but I thought an approach to this prospect could be profitable. At this time, I take out my phone and tell them that I have his phone number and that I am going to call him. I tell them that as soon as he answers, I will hand the phone to one of the salespersons and ask him to make an appointment to see the prospect. I ask the rest of the group to rate the body language of the person chosen as well as his effectiveness on the phone.

Usually, I can feel tension in the room as I walk around holding the phone. It gets almost unbearable when I actually start dialing. Then I will stop and ask how many of them were feeling that they would rather be somewhere else. At first, there is a nervous twittering and some smiles. I tell them that I will not do the exercise and put the phone away. At that stage, faces light up in relief and the release is definitely audible.

"How many of you," I ask, "would have preferred me to select someone other than you?" Most of the hands will go up.

This is a demonstration of Call Reluctance®. Just a few short minutes ago, everyone had declared their caring for their dealership and their sales careers. They knew that to advance their sales careers and their dealership, they should call on new prospects. Yet, when presented with the opportunity to do that very thing, they hesitated.

That hesitation is Call Reluctance®. Some may have hesitated because they were not comfortable doing the exercise in a group setting. Some may have hesitated because they did not think this was a professional way to call a prospect. Some may have hesitated because they did not feel properly prepared to make the call. Others may have hesitated because they were afraid they would upset the farmer with a cold call. There may even have been one or two who hesitated because it was my exercise and not their idea. The reasons for the hesitation are the different types of Call Reluctance®. There are 12 types and they all have at least one thing in common — they cause salespeople to avoid doing the things they already know how to do, say they want to do and are even motivated to do. And it costs.

The debris left in the wake of Call Reluctance® is stunning. Sometimes entire careers are ended because the salesperson was just not able to break through the Call Reluctance® barrier. Some careers are put on permanent hold because the salespersons do not understand what it is. Entire dealerships lose millions of dollars in sales that they could have had. They regularly default these sales to their competition.

Most dealerships explain it away as poor salespeople who are too lazy or who don't care enough for their careers. They blame apathy, lack of closing skills, easy sales and a whole host of other logical-sounding reasons.

Besides the lost sales, how much does Call Reluctance® cost a dealership? To answer this, you should look at the numbers of "astronaut equipment" sitting on dealer lots; these are equipment taken in trades that should never have happened at the prices they paid and that now take up space. You should also look at the number of times a salesperson, unable to say no, drops the price on a piece to the point where the dealership is lucky to come out even. You should look at the time wasted on non-business issues because the salesperson was not assertive enough to refuse to deliver the farmer's groceries. The cost is enormous.

WHICH CALL RELUCTANCES AFFECT DEALERS MOST?

In recent years, I have tested thousands of dealership personnel using the SPQ® Call Reluctance® Test. This remarkable instrument measures how much of each of the 12 types of Call Reluctance® is present in an individual. It also measures motivation and goal levels. The scores can tell you a great deal about what a salesperson is likely to do in a self-promotional situation. Unlike other psychological tests, this one does not reveal much about personality. Rather, it is what we call a "do" test - it tells you what someone will do. It predicts — very accurately — behaviors associated with selling.

Not surprisingly, farm equipment salespeople compare unfavorably with most other industries. Overall Call Reluctance® is more severe and there is more of it than in other salespeople.

Perhaps it's because it has been allowed to fester for so long. The most common Call Reluctance® in dealer salespeople is Yielder™ Call Reluctance®. This explains a lot of the behaviors that salespeople exhibit when faced with difficult customers. Stage Fright™ ranks very highly as does Telephobia™, Over-preparer™, Social Self-Consciousness™ and Oppositional Reflex™. Low goals is also a major problem.

WHAT DOES THIS MEAN?

What does this mean behaviorally? How do these Call Reluctances show themselves in practical terms? Let's examine them.

Yielder™ Call Reluctance® causes salespeople to constantly be yielding their own right of way to others. In a dealership, the Yielder™ salesperson finds it very difficult to say no, to walk away from an unprofitable deal or to stick to a price. Trying hard to be liked, he makes promises that he knows he cannot fulfill and creates unhappy customers as a result. Please understand that he wants happy customers. He simply creates dissatisfaction when he is unable to make good on his promises. He regularly and habitually avoids calling new prospects because he is afraid to upset them or to intrude on their time. He talks a good deal about bending over backwards for his customers and is even proud of it, especially when it has cost the dealership money. He uses this as an example of good service. He regularly walks away from unclosed deals because he did not have the courage to ask for the order. He wants his customers to "think about it" even when he knows there is nothing left to think about. He promises service work to the customer and then is afraid to tell the service manager about his concessions, leaving it to the service manager to discover it later on his own. He tells things to customers that he thinks they want to hear and then wonders why these customers go behind his back to get the real story from the technicians. He believes in relationship selling and forgets the reasons for the relationship.

Overpreparer Call Reluctance® causes salespeople to feel insecure about how much they know. The salesperson prepares more than is necessary and is slow to act. He tries to sell by inundating the customer with dry facts and technical specifications. He believes that information alone will make the sale and confuses customers. His sales presentations are normally devoid of emotion, and boring. He sends quote after quote, delighting in the prettiness of the quotation. To him, the more details he can provide, the likelier he is to sell. He lacks spontaneity and avoids situations where he feels inadequate. He gives up more sales than he makes.

Telephobia™ Call Reluctance® simply forces the salesperson to avoid making telephone calls to promote himself or the dealership. Calling for a pizza or his wife presents no problem. Cold calling on the telephone is taboo. He likens this to those pesky salespeople who call at night when you're having dinner. He wastes a tremendous amount of time shuffling prospect cards and just staring at the telephone After all, with modern technology, surely the telephone can make its own phone calls! He proudly states that he is more comfortable face-to-face than over the telephone. In an environment where customers are many miles apart, he prefers to gather windshield time rather than to pick up the telephone.

Social Self-Consciousness™ Call Reluctance® affects the dealer salesperson who has to call on wealthy farmers or corporate farms. Feeling inferior, he regularly avoids them. When he is forced to make the call, he becomes like a little child in their presence and fawns a lot. In one dealership in Montana, the salespeople told me of the many celebrities that had moved there and who had bought huge ranches or farms in their area. When asked how many of these they did business with, they looked at me as if I was stupid. It seems, according to them, these celebrities did not buy farm equipment. In a dealership in Idaho, the salespeople told me that most of the farms in their area were controlled by a handful of corporations. They did not deal with any of them because, according to them, the competition had already bought all of that business.

Stage Fright™ Call Reluctance® is a strange one. On the one hand, salespeople tell me they do not have to make group presentations. On the other hand, they admit that they should and that it could help them make more sales if they did. However, Stage Fright Call Reluctance® can affect salespeople when they must present to two or more people, such as the farmer and his wife. Suddenly, they have an audience and they become uncomfortable. A salesperson in Idaho once told me that he regularly dropped in at the local coffee shop where farmers gathered. He would select one farmer to make a sales pitch to. He did fine until the other farmers started to gather around and ask questions. That's when he became uncomfortable to the point where he would run for his pickup. "You won't believe the number of deals I left on the table in that coffee shop!" he told me.

Oppositional Reflex™ Call Reluctance® is perhaps the most destructive of all. This one causes salespeople to become belligerent when faced with customers who ask too many questions. For most salespeople, a question is welcomed as a request for more information. For the Oppositional, it represents an attack on his credibility. It's not that Oppositionals do not have the same on/off emotional switches that everyone else has. They do. They have simply lost the volume control. Small remarks become challenges. Any disagreement with their point of view becomes a declaration of war. Difficult to manage, they will not allow themselves to be coached or trained. They defy management, constantly issuing ultimatums. They become difficult to work with, contrary, and never feel part of the team. They have a tendency to act in opposites even when to do so is not in their best interests. They have to win senseless battles. They make customers mad or feel intimidated. They walk away from sales and then go back to the dealership and tell everyone there that the customer is not someone the dealership wants.

Low goals is a major problem for dealerships. Salespeople with low goals have no urgency. They display a lack of ambition. They tend to deflect the outcomes of their careers to upper management. They do not actively seek out any self-development. That is the responsibility of the sales manager. They complain often that the reason they are not doing well is because of management's lack of interest in them. They tend to do just enough to get by. They seem to lack any motivation to do more. They do not act empowered, even when told to do so. They get by with the minimum of activity but always look busy. Long-term targets hold no real interest for them. Neither do long-term rewards. They are more interested in getting something today even if it is far less than what they would receive later.

WHAT'S A SALES MANAGER TO DO?

The sales manager should properly understand Call Reluctance® and the implications of it in his sales force. Unfortunately, in most dealerships, the problem is too far along to wish it away. The sales manager is going to have to act. This action can come in two ways.

MANAGING IRON SALESPEOPLE

1. He should practice compensatory hiring. This means screening out new applicants who have Call Reluctance®.
2. He should test his salespeople for Call Reluctance® and, if it is severe, he should enroll them in a workshop to get rid of it. However, he must do the follow-up exercises with them and make sure that they do them properly. If he does not, he may waste more money and time.

    The sales manager should read the outstanding "bible" on Call Reluctance® — "Earning What You're Worth; the Psychology of Sales Call Reluctance©," by George W. Dudley and Shannon L. Goodson. This book is available from Sales Academy.

    One of the problems with ignoring Call Reluctance® is that it gets worse, not better, over time. Another problem is that all sales training becomes less effective. The Call Reluctance® that prevents the salesperson from making calls in the field, also prevents him from effectively learning new things in the classroom. In all the training that I design for my clients, I always include Call Reluctance® as the first step.

SIX COMBINES AND A SMILE!

Sam always knew there was something wrong. He had all the skills necessary to be a top equipment salesperson. He knew more about tractors and combines than anyone else in the dealership. Yet customers seemed to take great delight in deliberately making him mad. He often walked away from sales because he refused to put up with their nonsense. Sometimes, other salespeople in the dealership got his sales and that *really* made him mad. Other times, the dealership lost out to a competitor. Sam blamed those lost sales on the other dealer cutting prices. He refused to believe that he could be causing the problem.

When he attended the Call Reluctance® workshop and received his test report, he almost tore it up. It showed him to have a score of 87 on a scale called Oppositional Reflex™. He did not care about scores, he told himself, especially after the instructor told the class what Oppositional Reflex™ meant. For a few weeks, he stewed.

Walking away from another lost sale, he wondered, "What if the test was accurate after all?" Sam may have been oppositional but he was no fool. He got out his workshop material and started to read it all over again. He even toyed with doing the prescription he had received in the workshop. He felt that he had nothing to lose. The dealer was getting impatient with him.

Shrugging, he finally took the first major step. "I guess I am one of those," he thought. Then he threw himself into a cure called Fear Inversion. It was the most difficult thing Sam had ever done in his entire life but he stuck with it.

I know he did because he called me soon after he had completed it to tell me that he had just cracked a multi-unit deal and was on track to sell six combines that month. Then he called me again to tell me that he had sold all six.

He gave me some credit. "I guess you opened my eyes," he told me, "but I think I would have done it anyway."

I didn't care. Sam had made a breakthrough. He was never going to let a silly fear stop him ever again.

MANAGING IRON SALESPEOPLE

WHICH TYPE ARE YOU?
The 12 Types of Call Reluctance®

Doomsayer™ - These are salespeople who always see the worst-case scenario. They spend an enormous amount of time protecting themselves against fictional dangers. They find all sales more difficult than most.

Over-Preparer™ - These salespeople are afraid of appearing as if they do not know enough or are ill prepared. So they spend a great deal of time getting ready and will sacrifice opportunities in favor of preparation.

Hyper-Pro™ - These are over-concerned with projecting the right look or creating the right impressions. For them, looking right is often more important than doing right. They routinely avoid doing things they consider beneath them even if those same things have proven to be winners for the rest of the team. They talk a lot, always trying to demonstrate how clever they are. They have difficulty admitting mistakes.

Stage Fright™ - Salespeople with Stage Fright™ Call Reluctance® avoid group-selling situations. Sometimes two or more people comprise a group and they become increasingly uncomfortable and may even freeze up in some cases.

Role Rejection™ - These salespeople are secretly ashamed of being in sales. Although they have intellectually bought into selling as a worthwhile career, they still harbor emotional doubts about its worth. They tend to use up tremendous amounts of energy coping with their careers.

Yielder™ - These salespeople often hesitate because they are afraid of inciting conflict or imposing on others. They constantly yield their own right of way to others and then complain that they are taken advantage of. They regularly default many pieces of business to their competitors because they will not allow themselves to ask for the order.

Social Self-Consciousness™ - These salespeople are easily intimidated by others they consider better than themselves because of things such as wealth, power, position or even a better education. They routinely avoid calling on or dealing with these people.

Separationist™ - These people avoid doing business with their friends. Believing that business and friendships don't mix, they refuse to call on friends for business, or even help in finding new business. Repeat business from a client (now a friend) can be extremely difficult for them.

Emotionally Unemancipated™ - These people rule their families out as possible sources of new business or referrals.

Referral Aversion™ - Although they know how to get referrals, these salespeople tend to postpone asking for them, preferring to wait for a better time which never seems to come. Sales companies often misdiagnose this as a lack of training and spend enormous amounts of money teaching their salespeople how to ask for referrals. They already know how. They are simply emotionally unable to.

Telephobia™ - This is a very specific form of Call Reluctance®. It inhibits the use of the telephone when it comes to prospecting and self-promotion only. All other uses are allowed. Note - other types of Call Reluctance® can masquerade as Telephobia™. This is why an accurate assessment is needed.

Oppositional Reflex™ - This one is exactly what it sounds like. These people reflexively oppose. They tend to act in opposites even when to do so is not in their best interests. They become very difficult to manage, advise, train and coach. They critique often and become very defensive when challenged. Sales people with this type tend to fight with customers. They view customer inquiries as personal attacks on their credibility and they tend to lash out without thinking.

Why is Type Important?

Type is important because when you know what type you are dealing with, you can use very specific methods to eliminate it. Some procedures work very well with certain types but have no effect on others or could make them worse.

CHAPTER 11 - DO YOU WANT SUPERSTAR SALESPEOPLE?

There are already a few superstar salespeople in dealerships around the country. These are the ones who made the changes when they saw the writing on the wall. They have always been good salespeople. When technology started to play a major role in their industry, they did not wait around and complain. They learned the new technology and are today miles ahead of their competitors. They have carved a niche for themselves among their farmer clients. My hat goes off to these superstars.

For the sales manager who is wondering how to get them, it is too late. They are already spoken for. Can you turn your ordinary salespeople into superstars? Of course, you can. You may never be able to get them to think like superstars but, if you get them to do superstar behaviors on a daily basis, you can get them to perform like superstars.

There may be an easier way and that is to hire more wisely in the future.

MANAGING IRON SALESPEOPLE

WHAT TO LOOK FOR

The development of a superstar salesperson starts before the hiring process. The sales manager must have a clear idea of what he is looking for. He should take the time to study other successful salespeople in his industry to see what they have in common. He should examine his own feelings about salespeople and come up with traits or backgrounds that he would prefer.

Because of the complexity of the industry, one of the first things a sales manager should be looking for today is a higher education. This does not necessarily mean college graduates, though the trend is leaning toward them. The college graduate brings with him a proven ability to learn. If the person graduated with a major in farm economics or other agriculturally-related subjects, this could be a plus.

If I were a dealer, I would be looking for young, energetic salespeople. I would want someone who has the stamina and the work ethic to handle the long hours. I would also want the enthusiasm and malleability that comes with youth, though I would not rule out an older person who has the right qualifications. Youth brings with it a healthy ignorance — they have not yet learned that there are certain things that cannot be done.

The applicant should have a desire to be in this industry. This is not an industry that attracts young, ambitious salespeople. Therefore, a sales manager should examine the motivations of the applicants carefully. Where there is a genuine desire, this works in favor of the dealership.

The salesperson should show some ambition to make money and to develop a career in the dealership. While many dealerships do not offer much advancement potential, there is a great deal of money to be made by the right salespeople.

The applicant should already have good computer skills. Today, there is no longer any excuse for a reasonably educated person not to have these skills. While you may still have to train him on your programs, he should possess the skills that allow him to learn these quickly.

The potential sales superstar should be trainable. While self-assurance is a desirable asset, cockiness is not. The applicant should display a willingness to continue learning. In an older applicant, if the person indicates that he already knows it all, be careful.

Then there is chemistry. The sales manager must be able to get along with the salesperson. Unlike many huge companies where the person doing the hiring is not the person doing the managing, the sales manager in the dealership will be working with this salesperson daily. If they don't like each other, it can lead to a life of misery for both.

Of course, building on the last chapter, there should be no Call Reluctance® or low goals present. This is easily tested for. The SPQ® Call Reluctance® Test will tell the sales manager very clearly how much Call Reluctance® the applicant has and what his goal level is.

All of the above, with the exception of Call Reluctance®, can be observed and checked by the sales manager at the interview level.

WHERE TO FIND SALESPEOPLE

Placing ads in the local papers is always a good idea. However, the sales manager should not limit himself to the local area. There may be salespeople dissatisfied with outdated dealerships that are looking to improve their careers.

Internet advertising can become useful as time goes by. If your dealership has a web site, you can use this as a billboard.

If it does not, perhaps you should consider getting one pronto. If you are to attract top potential, your dealership needs to be on the cutting edge too.

Start scouting the college campuses for young graduates, especially those colleges that offer agricultural programs. Perhaps you can offer a third year student a part-time job in the dealership so that both of you can assess each other. Put him behind the parts counter. Let him travel with your best salespeople. Make him get his hands dirty in the shop. All this time, you can be observing him to see if there is a proper fit.

Talk to other dealers. If you belong to a Twenty Group, you can "advertise" the position among the members of this group. One of them may know of someone who is looking but does not have a position open and could refer the person to you. If your dealership is not part of a Twenty Group, you should be asking why. This is the most cost-effective learning a dealership can get. There are very few opportunities for dealer principals to advance their learning in practical terms. The Twenty Group provides this.

Talk to your employees. Let them know exactly what you are looking for and even offer a small reward if they recommend the right person to you.

Discuss it with your manufacturer's field representative. He usually has his ears to the ground and can often come up with the right candidate for you. He has a vested interest in making sure you get the right person. However, you should still make it clear what your parameters are. Field personnel become accustomed to dealers who look for the same type of people. They may not realize you are different.

YOU CAN TEST!
SPQ® - The Call Reluctance® Test

One of the most accurate psychometric assessments available is the SPQ® Call Reluctance® Test. Unlike most psychological tests that describe a personality ("are" tests), the SPQ® describes what a person is likely to do ("do" test) in certain self-promotional situations. This can be a very useful guide to a sales manager looking to hire a new sales superstar.

SPQ® measures motivation, goal level, goal diffusion and the 12 Call Reluctance® types. It helps to answer the 3 critical questions every sales manager should ask.

1. How much business is this new person likely to bring in that we don't already have?
2. How soon is this likely to happen?
3. At what cost?

These are business, not psychological, questions. These are the things that the sales manager will be judged on. If the answers to these questions do not conform to what the sales manager is looking for, then perhaps he should continue looking.

The SPQ® is a 110-question questionnaire with multi-choice answers. The applicant usually takes about 45 minutes of uninterrupted time to complete it. The answer sheet is scored by computer and a report generated.

The SPQ® is available from Sales Academy 1-800-898-3743. Tests are usually scored the same day they are received and a summary form with a management report is faxed to the dealership. The full report is mailed. Many dealers already use this as an important part of their hiring process.

THE INTERVIEW PROCESS

You do not have to hire the first applicant! While dealers often complain about how difficult it is to find personnel, you should always consider the consequences of hiring the wrong salesperson.

Because this is such an important position, you will want to use some testing instruments like the SPQ®. So many sales managers have told me that they do not need testing. They rely on their own instincts. Think about this. When you hire a skilled builder to build your house, how comfortable would you be if he did not use tools to measure the building he will build for you? Test early. It can save you a great deal of time.

It is always better for more than one person to interview applicants at different times. The sales manager may overlook some things that another manager may spot. There are many books written about the interview process. Read them and learn to look for the right things and to ask the right questions. Make sure you do not run afoul of the equal opportunity laws of your state.

One thing you should always do in the interview: Make sure that the applicant understands what is expected of him. These expectations should be spelled out clearly and should include behavioral expectations such as planning and cold calling.

Compare applicants and then decide on the best one for you. If none of the applicants suit you, start the search all over again. In the life of a dealership, an extra month or two is not critical.

EARLY PERFORMANCE

The best predictor of future sales success is early performance. If you take 10 new hires and rank them in order of their performance at the end of three months and then rank them again at the end of 12 months, you will find that the order has not changed much. There will be some exceptions but the general order will be similar. If one salesperson is in the top quarter at the end of three months, he will likely be in the top quarter at the end of 12. If he is in the bottom quarter at the end of three months, the chances are high that that's where he will be nine months later. This is based on research done by George W. Dudley, co-author of the Call Reluctance® program.

What this tells you is that the best chance any salesperson has for future success is determined by how quickly he starts. This is more reliable as a predictor of sales success than any test you can buy.

It also tells you that your best chance of developing a sales superstar is to make sure that he starts quickly. Get him successful as quickly as you can. Design his sales career in such a way that you get him out there selling successfully fast. Do this and you have increased your chances tremendously.

WHERE ARE ALL THE EMPLOYEES?

So many dealers have told me how difficult it is to find qualified employees and I believe them. However, I think the situation can often be exaggerated.

A Washington dealer told me he had tremendous difficulty finding employees because the town where the dealer was located was small. Yet, when I examined how long his employees had been with him, I found that more than half of them had been there less than two years. I asked if he had grown dramatically over the past two years and he said no. This meant that, in this dealership of about 25 employees, he had lost and found 12 new employees in two years.

Where did they come from? According to him, this dealership should have closed down because of the number of employees lost that, according to most dealers, cannot be replaced.

CAREER PATHS

One of the biggest benefits of multi-store operations is that they offer career opportunities for all employees. In a smaller operation, there can only be one sales manager. For the salesperson to be promoted to this position, the sales manager has to be promoted, retire or die. Not so in larger dealerships.

If your dealership has the opportunity to promote, you should map out the career of the new salesperson from the start. Let him know what the opportunities are and what he will need to do to earn them. Make sure that you have thought this out carefully. You want to avoid changing career paths in midstream because of your own lack of proper planning.

If your dealership is unable to offer career advancement opportunities, you can still map out a career path for the new salesperson. Instead of promotion possibilities, there can be graduating degrees of commissions, expanded territories, a say in the development of marketing plans, or other opportunities. Don't forget that, if he does well in the territory you assign him, he will create opportunities for additional salespeople. If you hire additional salespeople as a result of his efforts, then he could have a say in the hiring of the new salespeople as well as share in the rewards in the form of an overriding commission if he helps to train the new salesperson. Again, make sure he understands the conditions under which he will advance and what will happen if he does not.

In a smaller store, you want to make the new salesperson feel part of the team. You want him to take ownership of his career. Give him the right opportunities and he may just do that.

CHAPTER 12 - WHAT DO YOU EXPECT FROM YOUR SALESPEOPLE?

In this chapter, we are going to look in depth at expectations. When you are hiring a new salesperson, you have an ideal opportunity to list your expectations. When dealing with a veteran sales force, the sooner you lay out your expectations, the better. You should always look at behavioral expectations — what should they do? This is different from setting targets.

WHAT DO YOU WANT YOUR SALESPEOPLE TO DO?

If you answered "to sell," go to the back of the class and hide your face.

If you want your salesperson to succeed, you must first define what success means to you. Most sales managers talk about success in terms of the number of sales a salesperson completes consistently. They usually add in customer satisfaction and repeat customers. They tell this to their salespeople and feel that they have now laid out their expectations. I'm going to ask you to go a few steps further.

How will your salespeople accomplish repeat, consistent sales? The answer is remarkably simple. They need to perform very simple successful behaviors consistently. What these successful behaviors are depends on the sales manager. He should not only define which successful behaviors will move his salespeople closer to their targets, he should quantify them. How many of each should they ideally do on a consistent basis? The performance of these successful behaviors will determine how close they get to their targets.

This means that the sales manager must not only define and quantify the successful behaviors, he must also manage them. He must make sure that his salespeople do them regularly and consistently. He should monitor them to make sure they produce the right results.

He can make mistakes! In setting up the successful behaviors, the sales manager could make mistakes and this really is not critical to success. He can always change them as he discovers his mistakes. He can delete them completely, change the frequency or alter the method of doing them.

What are some examples of successful behaviors? My other book, *"P.A.S.S. C.A.L.F. - 8 Behaviors of Sales Success in an Agricultural Dealership,"* lists eight in some detail. That may be a good starting point. The sales manager should add his own.

The successful behaviors should apply to every salesperson in the dealership. There should be no exceptions. However, they can be tailored to each individual. A good method is to interview each salesperson one-on-one and ask him what he thinks he should do consistently to make the sales that you have jointly agreed upon. The sales manager can guide them to come up with their own formula for success. These successful behaviors will be in addition to the basic ones already in force for all salespeople.

The sales manager should be careful to steer the

salesperson away from attitudes. By definition, successful behaviors are *actions*, not attitudes. So, being positive is not a successful behavior. It is useful, of course, but it does not constitute a behavior. You cannot measure it or even quantify it. However, coming to work with a smile and greeting everyone cheerfully can be a successful behavior.

Once the successful behaviors have been defined for each salesperson, the sales manager should ask, "How can we know that you are doing these?" There should be a report-back system that allows the sales manager to know that these successful behaviors are being performed. He should also devise a method for evaluating the effectiveness of these behaviors.

CAN THEY DO IT?

My friend and training superstar, Bob Hilleque, does an exercise that illustrates graphically the difference between skill versus attitude. It goes like this.

- If I asked you to fly me from point A to point B, could you do it?

The answer depends on whether or not you have the skills needed to pilot a plane. That's obvious. However, regardless of skills, you could still stay no. You could simply refuse based on your attitude. How do I know the difference?

- If I put a gun to your head and threatened to kill you if you did not fly me from point A to point B, what would your answer now be?

If your life depended on it, you might try but would probably get both of us killed anyway. If you genuinely did not know how to pilot a plane, your answer would be, "You might as well shoot me now because I don't know how to fly a plane." If you did know how to fly a plane, you would take me from point A to point B.

The difference is skill versus attitude. (Sorry, Bob, I probably didn't do your exercise justice.)

There are salespeople who would do what you want if only they knew how to do it. In this case, training is needed to get them to do it. On the other hand, there are salespeople who refuse to do what you want because of reasons other than their ability to perform. This requires a closer look. It could be because of Call Reluctance®. We know that this limits the salesperson's ability to perform regardless of skill. It could also be a totally negative attitude that may require some adjusting.

Very often, as Bob points out, the sales manager does not take the time to discern the difference. If a salesperson does not perform, he automatically assumes that more training is needed. He then becomes disillusioned with training when it does not cure the problem.

NON-NEGOTIABLE BEHAVIORS

Certain behaviors cannot be tolerated in a dealership. These are what we term non-negotiable behaviors. There is no negotiation. They are simply unacceptable.

For example, your salesperson makes an appointment to see a customer and then decide to take the day off and go fishing instead. That's not acceptable. Or he deliberately lies to the customer. That's not acceptable. The sales manager should define what the non-negotiable behaviors of his sales force are. He should make sure all salespeople know what these are and take action whenever they transgress.

There should be very clear consequences for non-negotiable behaviors. Notice, I said consequences and not punishment. There is a difference. If you are caught speeding, the police officer who pulls you over does not punish you for it. Instead, he calmly gives you a ticket. This ticket is the consequence of your behavior. There is nothing personal in this. He will even avoid arguing with you. He simply hands you a ticket. When you get in front of a judge, that's a different story. He metes out punishment.

The sales manager should avoid trying to punish salespeople. Punishment has no place in the work environment. Instead, he should have clear rules for consequences that the salespeople should understand. Here is a guideline given to managers in my Successful Dealer Behaviors Program:

NON-NEGOTIABLE OR UNACCEPTABLE BEHAVIORS

The following behaviors are not acceptable in my department and are not negotiable:

1..
2..
3..
4..

A WAY OF DEALING WITH NON-NEGOTIABLE BEHAVIORS

1. Always make sure all employees know that these behaviors are unacceptable.
2. The first time employees behave unacceptably, speak to them

MANAGING IRON SALESPEOPLE

immediately and make sure they understand that the behavior is not acceptable to you. Perhaps they did not know.
3. The second time employees do the same non-negotiable behavior, give them a written warning and let them know they will only receive two such written warnings before more drastic action will be taken.
4. The third time employees do the same non-negotiable behavior, give them a second written warning and let them know this is the last written warning they will receive.
5. The fourth time employees do the same non-negotiable behavior, give them a day off with half pay. They should regard this as a career day to decide if they want to continue employment with you. If they do, they will come to work the next day as if nothing had happened and continue working. This will be an agreement that they will no longer do the non-negotiable behavior.
6. The fifth time employees do the same non-negotiable behavior, give them 3 days off without pay for them to evaluate themselves and their positions on the team. They should have a meeting with you when they return. You should then clearly outline the consequences of their continuing the behavior. The next time, they will have self-terminated.
7. Perform all the above steps without emotion. Do not get into a mudslinging match. Just simply state the behavior and the consequences.
8. If you have followed the above and the employee still does not conform to acceptable behavior, he has sent you a very clear message – he does not want to be part of your team.
9. Remember, as long as you are coaching, they are part of your team. When you stop coaching, they have already left your team.

    One dealer told me he agreed with the above except that he

would have fired the employee after the third occasion. I agreed with him. However, this behavior policy was written for all departments where it is sometimes difficult to replace personnel and this allows every effort to be made to save the employee. I am a firm believer in trying your best to save an employee until there is no longer any hope.

HOW NEGOTIABLE ARE YOU?

Here are some true examples of behaviors in dealerships that I have told many times.

1. A partsperson arrives at work around noon instead of at 7.30 am like everyone else. Since it is now lunchtime, he unpacks his Big Mac, fries and coke and starts to have lunch at the parts counter. There are customers waiting but he ignores them. When a customer dares to interrupt his lunch, he asks the customer to come back later, after lunch.

2. A technician is sent out to a customer who has broken down in the field during harvest. On his way, he decides that he does not feel like working anymore that day and goes fishing instead. The service manager finds out when the irate farmer calls to find out where the technician is. The next day, the technician clocks in as if nothing has happened.

3. A salesperson keeps a small fridge in his office at the dealership. In it, he has a store of goodies to eat that he sells to the employees at a profit. He has a nice little side business in the dealership. For about two hours during the lunch periods, he is not available since he is too busy selling food.

4. Three technicians become unhappy when their dealership merges with another. They visit the farmer customers to get a petition signed to close down the new dealership. When the

> **HOW NEGOTIABLE ARE YOU? (Continued)**
>
> customers refuse to become involved, they make veiled threats (and some not so veiled) about damaging their equipment. They send the petition to the president of the manufacturer.
>
> If you were the dealer, would you accept such behaviors? Would you believe it if I told you that, in every case, the dealers did? In two cases, relatives of the owner carried out the behaviors. I'll bet you would not guess which two.
>
> While many dealers talk about not accepting certain non-negotiable behaviors, their non-action tells a different story. For them, everything is negotiable and their employees know it.

SETTING GOALS

We spoke about setting targets in an earlier chapter. In this chapter, we spoke about setting behavioral expectations. Now let's look at goals. Are they different? Yes.

Targets are what you set as a business necessity. Behavioral expectations are what salespeople need to do to reach those targets. Goals are more personal.

Back in 1996, I developed a "Goals Achievement" workshop and delivered it to about 2500 dealer personnel at the John Deere Company Expo in San Antonio. In preparation for this workshop, I attended many goal setting workshops. I did not go to learn how to set goals but to observe the participants. At some stage in every workshop, the instructor would ask participants to write down their goals. This seemed a simple enough exercise. I noticed that there were some people who struggled enormously with this while others had no difficulty at all.

As the instructor walked around the room, some scribbled furiously in their note books. Some covered up their note books as they wrote furtively but not a lot. Some sat looking into space until the instructor noticed them and then they pretended to write something down. For some, this exercise held enormous hope while for others it seemed to scare the heck out of them. I wondered why.

Further study and my own experiments showed me at least part of the answer. Some people have no difficulty when it comes to setting goals. They relish the idea and write down their goals easily. They then paste these goals in a place that will remind them of what they want. This inspires them to achieve those goals.

There are others George Dudley calls "goal-aversive". As soon as they write down their goals, they become afraid of those very goals. Placing them in a prominent place actually has a detrimental effect on them.

There are those I call "goal-depressed". They have never learned how to set goals; they go through life aimlessly and without direction.

Then there are some people who, like me, don't seem to need goals. I call these people "goal-immune". Ask them where they will be in a year and they have difficulty with the answer. Some don't even know where they will be next month. If you ask them if they have goals, they say, "of course," but they have difficulty in telling you exactly what these are. Yet they can be highly successful. I discovered some time ago that I fell into this category. I have never written down my goals and have great difficulty explaining them even to myself. But I have a direction and, as long as I keep my eye on that direction, I feel I am accomplishing things important to me.

The other part of the goal-setting workshops I attended that seemed awkward, happened when the instructor asked the participants to write down the things they needed to do to get to their goals. I felt that this was premature. Every instructor automatically assumed that the "goals" the participants had written down were real goals, that these were things they really wanted.

In talking to many participants of these workshops, I realized something else. Many of them had never defined what a goal was for them. Usually, the things they wrote down as goals were nothing more than vehicles for getting them to the things they really wanted. The real goals only came after many questions and then they were ethereal, almost mystical. I would ask participants, "Why do you want that?" over and over again until we reached a goal that often had no logic or sense. That was the real goal.

Then, having stated the real goal, they could choose many different vehicles to reach it. Once they had chosen the right vehicle, it really became a simple thing to put their plan into operation.

This led me to believe that goal *setting* is only one small step in the *goals achievement* process. There are four steps.

1. Define what a goal is.
2. Set the goal. This is a 3-step process.
   A. You must know what you want.
   B. You must be able to articulate it in clear terms.
   C. You must know why it is important.
3. Develop a strategy for getting there.
4. Put the strategy into action immediately - The Nike step: *Just do it!*

Although I do not personally have clear goals, I believe everyone has something he wants to achieve. When you can uncover this something, you can use it to help the person create successful behaviors to achieve it. Therefore, in my opinion, goals are very personal things and not the targets businesses set.

This is where the sales manager comes in. Each of your salespeople will have something personal that they would like to achieve in their lives, something that is important to them. If you can tie their goals to your targets, perhaps you will both get what you want. Show them how, by performing the successful behaviors you set for them, they can also reach their personal goals.

Much is made of motivating employees. Whole industries have grown up around this theme. I believe that employees can best be motivated by using their own goals to do it. Why bother? Well, for one thing, all businesses are interested in customer satisfaction. I believe that satisfied customers start with satisfied employees and employee satisfaction stems from the fulfillment of their goals, or at least the expectation that their goals will be fulfilled.

If you can tie their goals to career behaviors that will move them closer to their goals, you have a better chance of motivating them. If one of the vehicles for getting to their goals is the job you offer them, then it makes sense for them to use this job wisely. Non-negotiable behaviors can get them fired and slow their progress towards their goals. Successful behaviors can get them noticed, promoted or more money. This can move them closer to their goals.

The sales manager who takes the time to uncover the personal goals of his salespeople and then aligns their goals with his will have discovered the magic key to the motivation puzzle.

MANAGING IRON SALESPEOPLE

HOW IMPORTANT IS MONEY?

A 2000 national survey showed that only a small percentage of people in the USA wants to be very wealthy. This confused the capitalists, Republicans and others who had assumed for years that everyone in America wanted the "American Dream" and this always included a lot of money. I listened to a talk show host denounce those not wanting wealth as being less than ambitious. To hear him describe them in his condescending tone, they were the Liberals who were out to destroy America and all it stood for.

Perhaps he was just too taken up with his own ideals. I have done study after study in dealerships. The results bear out the survey with one exception. In dealerships, wealth is ranked as important by a much smaller percentage of the people. Do you want to know what they ranked way ahead of money?

1. Time with family
2. Education for their children
3. A reasonable salary and respect came in jointly for third place.

Wealth was way down on the list.

CHAPTER 13 - ESSENTIALS FOR SALESPEOPLE

Since this is not a sales training manual, I am not going to go into great depth about sales training. However, in today's dealership, there are certain essentials that the sales manager should make sure are in place to create better sales and ensure the longevity of the dealership.

1. GET TO KNOW THE CUSTOMER

This is the responsibility of the salesperson. This cannot be stressed enough. As farming becomes more complicated and machinery becomes more sophisticated, the farmer will rely more on the expertise of the dealer salesperson. For the salesperson to be fully effective, he will have to take the time to learn the business of his customer. If he does not, the customer will be forced to live without him. There are too many salespeople in dealerships already who don't know enough to give reliable advice to their farmer customers. For them, it's only a matter of time before the farmer cuts them out of his circle.

Knowing the customer's business is more than knowing how much land he farms or what he raises. It is understanding the problems he faces on a daily basis and knowing how to resolve or lessen those problems for him. It means knowing more about his business than the competition does and being able to apply that knowledge to practical solutions for him. This knowledge does not come from simply chatting to the farmer. Nor does it come through osmosis. The salesperson has to devote his time on a planned basis to learn the things he needs to learn. It does not mean that he should know more about the farmer's business than the farmer. After all, the dealer salesperson is a specialist. He should know how to apply his specialty to the needs of his farmer customers.

I recommend that any salesperson spend a day each quarter working on the farm of one of his best customers. If he positions this correctly, he will not be milking cows or shoveling manure all day. He will be in a position to add to his store of knowledge about this farmer. He should let the farmer know why he wants to do this and ask that the farmer arrange for him to observe first-hand different aspects of the business.

The benefits are enormous. First, there is the knowledge gained. Second, there is the farmer's perception that the salesperson really cares about his business. Imagine what he will tell his neighbors and other farmers. Third, it creates a more solid bond between the farmer and the salesperson. It makes it more difficult for the competition to disrupt the relationship. Cutting prices will then become the only weapon the competition has.

2. PROFILES

Profiles are an ideal way for the salesperson to get to know the customer's business. The salesperson who refuses to collect good, solid profiles and update them regularly will never get to the same level as the salesperson who does.

The sales manager should make the collection of profiles on targeted top customers a non-negotiable behavior. The sales manager should also teach the salespeople how to read and analyze a profile for future business. He should involve everyone in the dealership in the profile. After all, it does benefit every department.

FREE PROFILE!

The sales manager should create his own dealership profile form for his salespeople. Those supplied by manufacturers are inadequate for the purpose. Even the one created by Sales Academy is not specific enough for every dealership, though it does go way beyond the manufacturer's profile form.

For a limited time, Sales Academy will give free to every dealership that requests one, a copy of the profile it created for dealerships.

To get your copy, simply email me at franklee@sales-academy.com or send a fax requesting a free profile to 972-874-2864. You should specify whether you would like this on disk (Word97) or a hard copy.

With this at hand, you can create your own dealership profile.

---

3. KNOW THE COMPETITION

Since competitors are a fact for all dealers, salespeople should know as much as possible about them. The sales manager can help by gathering information on competitive dealers and competitive equipment and make sure the salespeople know how to access this information and use it. The salespeople should be actively involved in collecting this data.

On a regular basis, the sales manager should bring in a competitive model and demonstrate to the salespeople the differences between it and the ones they sell. They should not only learn the differences but also how to best present those differences without demeaning the competition.

In sales meetings, the sales manager should play "what if?" games with his salespeople. "What if I were the competitor and came in on your deal? What could I do to swing the customer away from you to me? How would you respond?" He should make sure the responses are based on solid competitor knowledge and not simply guesswork.

The salespeople should become so knowledgeable about the competition that they become the first source of reference for the competitor's customers. This will really drive the competition crazy.

4. SELL THROUGH THE EYES OF THE CUSTOMER

Salespeople often make the mistake of trying to sell iron. They know they have to meet certain equipment targets and so they go searching for customers who will buy that equipment. When used equipment builds up to intolerable levels, the sales manager tells them they had better move some of that lot rot, or else. They go knocking on doors, saying, "I've got a used baler. Do you want it?"

If salespeople are ever to raise their levels in dealerships, the sales manager has to teach them to look at things through the eyes of the customer. Instead of pushing iron, they should be asking themselves, "Why should this customer buy this? What problems will it solve?"

Instead of delivering a superlative presentation on the features, advantages and benefits of a piece of equipment, they should ask the farmer why he would buy it and concentrate on his use, not theirs.

When salespeople start to look at things through the eyes of the customer, they stop some of the time-wasting and outdated things they do. Instead of just dropping in for a bit of jawing, they call the customer with a valid business reason and make a definite appointment to talk about something of interest to the farmer. Instead of starting out with price, they find the reasons why the farmer would want the machine at almost any price.

FARM PRACTICES MEETINGS

Bill Fogarty, Editor Emeritus for Farm Equipment Magazine, asked me:

"What would you say about a salesman/sales manager participating in farm practices meetings? Periodically, I have heard farmers, ag educators and others remark about how seldom one sees equipment dealers and/or their salespeople at certain kinds of farmer meetings. This could include meetings of the conservation district. It could be a chemical or fertilizer supplier having an educational meeting. Maybe it will be the county agent explaining how a new USDA program will work. Will they be talking about equipment — changing practices that require changing equipment? Maybe or maybe not. But they'll be talking about farming — about new ideas. Is it worth keeping track of, and demonstrating concern?"

My answer is a resounding, *"Yes!"* In my *Most Valued Customer Workshop*, I teach salespeople how to make themselves more visible in the community and how to develop a network of resources. Bill is right. This is another resource available to the dealer salesperson.

They start to treat the customer the way they would want to be treated if they owned the farm. They practice "opportunity listening". They are always looking for ways to help the farmer to do better business. And they put their own pride in their pocket. It becomes less important that they look good than that the customer feels good.

Looking through the eyes of the customer does not mean giving in to the whims of the customer. It means understanding the relationship from the customer's point of view and doing the right things to maintain and grow the relationship — all the time through the customer's eyes.

The sales manager should actively encourage this type of approach to sales. In sales meetings, he should often ask, "If you were the customer, is that what you would want?" He should force his salespeople to answer the question. I have dealt with many, many salespeople in dealerships and found that this concept is one of the most difficult for them to fully understand and practice. They pay lip service to it in workshops but conveniently forget it in the field.

The sales manager can make sure that they practice it by constantly challenging them on it and consistently keeping it in front of them.

When salespeople do the essentials as outlined above and become good at them, they bewilder the competition. They also develop relationships with their customers that are profitable and long-lasting.

A MORE NATURAL SELLING PROCESS

One of my colleagues in Singapore, Galen Chay, has developed a role-play exercise for one of my sales workshops. He selects one person to be the salesperson, one person to be the customer and the rest of the team to be observers. He then instructs the salesperson to sell to the customer but with one caveat — he is not allowed to ask any questions.

The presentation is always stiff and unnatural. Eventually, the salesperson will complain that he cannot do it without asking some questions. The customer will complain that the salesperson does not understand what he wants and the observers will say that this is not the way they would do it.

Asking questions and getting inside the customer's head and seeing things through his eyes is actually a more natural way to sell. Salespeople just seem to forget to do it expertly or enough times.

CHAPTER 14 - MANAGING SUCCESSFUL BEHAVIORS

How can the sales manager effectively manage the successful behaviors of his salespeople? After all, they will readily agree with him that these are proper behaviors for them and, if performed, will make them money and raise their levels as salespeople. They will even promise to perform them.

Unfortunately, acceptance, agreement and promises do not always result in action. This is where the sales manager can really earn his salary. He can get them to actually do them. How? By making them part of the selling process.

Instead of relying on promises, the sales manager should require proper reporting that demonstrates that the behaviors have been done and allows him to evaluate the results. Here is a method I have used successfully in dealerships.

1. Get the agreement on the successful behaviors from the salespeople. They must buy into the behaviors or else they will resist every step of the way. This is where the sales

MANAGING IRON SALESPEOPLE

manager demonstrates his own selling ability. He must sell the successful behaviors to the salespeople.
2. Once agreement has been reached, he must make the successful behaviors non-negotiable. Although he may have personalized some of the behaviors for different salespeople, none are exempt from performing them. Consequences for nonperformance must be clearly spelled out.
3. In a veteran sales force, it may be necessary to take "baby steps". Start with one behavior and make sure this is done every week for four weeks. Then add another that will be used concurrently for the next four weeks. Then add two more and so on.
4. Develop a reporting form. This should be very simple since it adds to the paperwork that salespeople generally hate. Completion and return of the reporting form also becomes a non-negotiable behavior. For an example of a reporting form, see page 139.
5. Let the salespeople know that the behaviors are cumulative and demonstrate how they will be applied.

USING THE BEHAVIOR FORM

Each Monday, the sales manager hands each salesperson a successful behavior form and makes sure the salesperson understands what is required to complete it. During the week, the salesperson will perform the successful behavior or behaviors on the form. At the end of the week, the salesperson hands the completed form back to the sales manager.

It is up to the sales manager to make sure the completed forms are returned each Friday. If he lets it slip, the salespeople will too. I often have to remind managers that they may have to baby sit their people for the first few weeks until these forms become part of the process and habitual.

It should be pointed out that the sales manager should not begin this process if he does not intend to continue it. He could do more harm to his salespeople if he does. Why? Because he will have shown them that he is not serious about their development and his decisions on dealer development are based on how he feels each month. He has just added to the "flavor-of-the-month" syndrome seen in many dealerships. It will also make it more difficult the next time he has a bright idea.

For a sales manager to institute and then manage successful behaviors, he must be committed to his salespeople and care enough about their development to take the extra time and effort to do this. He must also believe in the process himself. If he does not, he will drop it at the first salesperson complaint.

Whenever I help dealers begin this process, the first complaints come from the salespeople. A common complaint is, "Do you want me to sell or complete forms?" My answer is a very simple, "Yes."

WHAT HAPPENS WHEN YOU FORGET?

Managers tend to forget because of all the other things that crop up. When they do, they let their people down. When they let the forms slip for a few weeks, it becomes very difficult to get it started again. Why? Their people have learned that these were not as important as they had been led to believe in the first place. Their managers had demonstrated this very clearly to them.

When this happens, I also have to remind managers that this is not a catch-up program. In other words, behaviors that have not been performed are lost forever. One cannot go back and ask the people to perform past behaviors to catch up. The manager has to start all over again. Managers become embarrassed when this happens because they have demonstrated that they do not care about their people as much as they had indicated. They tend to want to cover this embarrassment by pretending it had not happened or by blaming someone or something else. There is only one way to credibly save the program at this stage and that is for the manager to accept responsibility for this failure and promise his people that he will not let them down again.

I developed a program for dealerships called the Successful Dealer Behaviors Program. In this program, all department managers create and manage successful behaviors for their people.

In one dealership where I did the Successful Dealer Behaviors Program, the managers did not keep their end of the deal. Instead of accepting responsibility, they blamed it on the program. One of the managers called me to tell me that the program was not working because their people were complaining about their test reports. The manager told me there were people who were questioning the accuracy of the reports. He said the problem was widespread. This was, naturally, of concern to me. I asked the manager to arrange for me to meet with each of the employees in question and he agreed to do this. I made a two-day trip to this dealership to meet individually with these people. When I arrived, I was surprised to find that he had set up only three appointments. He sheepishly told me that it was not as widespread as he had imagined.

When I met the three employees, they told me that they did not question the test results. They used that as an excuse to get to talk to me. They were questioning the sincerity of their managers. They told me that they had been performing the behaviors asked of them and were seeing tremendous results. Then their managers stopped handing out the behavior forms. Even when the employees asked for their forms, their managers kept forgetting. The three employees had been asked by the other employees to do something about it and so they had complained about their test reports and asked to talk to me about them. This was the only way, they claimed, that they could have gotten proper attention. They wondered if their managers cared as much about the dealership as they did.

When I reported this back to the managers, they admitted that they were at fault and blamed it on the busy season. I could see that they would continue to bring up excuses for their own lack of commitment. We finally fixed the problem but not until the managers re-committed to their employees.

P.A.S.S. C.A.L.F. - 8 BEHAVIORS OF SALES SUCCESS IN AN AGRICULTURAL DEALERSHIP

When I wrote this book, it was intended as a text book for my Behavioral Sales Workshop for dealer salespeople and their managers. It worked very well in this workshop. I did not foresee how successful it would become as a sale item. Dealers from all over the United States and Canada purchased several thousand copies. One of the neatest things for me was when a dealer would order one copy and then call back later and order several more. When a professor from a college in Missouri called to request permission to use it as a text book in an agricultural business class, I was delighted.

How can a sales manager use this book in the dealership? I think it is a mistake to just give it to his salespeople and ask them to read it. This book was not meant just to be read. It was meant to show salespeople in dealerships what to do. After all, they can agree all they want about the benefits of the eight behaviors described in the book. If they do not put them into practice, they will not get much value from it.

> ### BABY STEPS
>
> When we develop "baby step" behaviors in our Successful Dealer Behaviors Program, one behavior I encourage is to have technicians clean their work stalls each Friday before going home. This is such an elementary behavior but one that is often allowed to get out of hand in a dealership. The service manager will almost always comment, "Boy, wouldn't that be nice!"
>
> When I read the behavior forms that they return, I find that this is something the technicians themselves want. Here are some comments from the behavior forms.
>
> - "It's a pleasure to work in a clean shop."
> - "The customers seem to appreciate a cleaner, more professional looking shop."
> - "We should do this more often."
> - "The shop is safer now."
> - "I feel proud about working here."
>
> Everyone knew that this was something that ought to be done. Everyone wanted it. Yet nobody took the responsibility to make sure it got done. We sometimes overlook things like this because we get into the habit of not doing them. Then we start doing them and everyone thinks it is something brand new.
>
> After a short while, this "baby step" becomes habit and the technicians feel very uncomfortable when the shop is left dirty.

Instead, the sales manager should assign one behavior to two salespeople and ask them to read the chapter that deals with this behavior. They should then come to the next sales meeting to explain it. One salesperson should explain the behavior and demonstrate why it is worthwhile for them to perform it. The other salesperson should come with an argument against it. The sales manager should allow them to debate the behavior and have the other salespeople take sides. If the final consensus is that the behavior is worth practicing, they should put it into immediate use and agree to report on the effectiveness of the behavior in the field.

The sales manager can then move to the next behavior and keep going until all the behaviors are covered. The salespeople should also be encouraged to come up with their own successful behaviors that they feel would benefit them and the other salespeople.

This may seem like a very slow process. But remember, the salespeople have already developed some unproductive habits and may not be ready for a complete makeover. By concentrating on one behavior at a time and getting them to perform this behavior, the sales manager has a better chance of eventually getting them to perform all the behaviors. Besides, if he continues this exercise long enough, he will have started to change the way the salespeople view selling. He will have gotten them to understand and accept the need to perform simple successful behaviors consistently and he will have developed successful habits in his salespeople.

The sales manager should not move to another behavior until the one in question has been thoroughly explored and given a fair chance. This does not mean perfecting it. He is not looking for perfect salespeople. He is looking for effective salespeople. They can be effective without being perfect.

If one of the behaviors proves ineffective for the salespeople, abandon it. Nowhere in the book does it say that the behaviors will work for every salesperson or every dealership. However, before abandoning it, the sales manager may try to alter it to suit the dealership. If this does not work, then abandon it and move to the next one or come up with a different one.

In creating their own successful behaviors, salespeople

should be reminded that these are *actions*, not attitudes. One must be able to see the behavior being done and one must be able to measure the effectiveness of it.

Successful Behavior Form

(NAME OF DEALERSHIP)

SALESPERSON SUCCESSFUL ACTION FORM

ACTION: ....

SALESPERSON: ....

STORE: ....

DATE: ....

RESULT OF ACTION: ....

....

INSTRUCTIONS:
1. ....

2. ....

3. ....

HAND THIS FORM BACK TO THE SALES MANAGER BY FRIDAY

CHAPTER 15 - SALES TRAINING

    A sales manager can go several ways when it comes to sales training. This chapter will not advocate one over another. I believe all sales training has value. The only sales training I am not altogether happy with is off-the-shelf, generic or canned sales training. Often, this type of training is too full of theory or contains too many situations that do not apply to the salespeople being trained.

    The sales manager should examine the deficiencies in skill and behaviors of his salespeople and devise training that addresses them. Customized sales training, although initially more expensive, tends to deliver more. In the long term, this type of training is much more economical because it is far more specific to the salespeople. It usually contains very little theory and relies more on real-life scenarios that the salespeople face on a daily basis. This type of sales training has little flab and keeps the attention of the salespeople much more effectively because they can relate to it. Unfortunately, most sales managers in dealerships are unable to develop this type of training and so they must look to outside consultants to do it for them. I believe that this is an investment in the future of the dealership. Properly developed, a customized sales training program should be able to be used for many years for all new hires.

It makes sense that the person or company developing this type of training must have an in-depth knowledge of the dealership and the industry or at least be willing to acquire this knowledge before developing a sales training program. The sales manager should examine the credentials of the consultant and ask for several references.

Many dealerships rely on their manufacturers for training. When it comes to sales training, however, manufacturers may not be the ideal source. The people responsible for developing or acquiring the sales training for their dealers are very often not salespeople themselves. Most are trainers or human resource personnel. I have seen executives of one manufacturer debate about what a salesperson *is* for over a year while they were trying to find a sales training program for their dealers. This does not mean that the manufacturer cannot come up with a good sales training program. Given enough time, they could. The sales manager should simply scrutinize the sales training program they offer the same way he would scrutinize any other, applying the same standards. If it passes, this could be the most cost-effective way to go.

In this chapter, I am going to look at the various kinds of training that the sales manager should consider for his salespeople.

FORMAL EDUCATION

While an advanced formal education has never been the determining factor in whether or not a salesperson will be successful, it certainly does help. In today's dealership, it is becoming more important to acquire salespeople with a college degree. The degree should preferably be in either an ag-related field or in business. This does not necessarily make them better salespeople. What it does is demonstrate that they have an ability to learn. It equips them to better understand the new technologies of the industry and to put these to practical uses for their customers.

Today's farmer is more educated and will feel more comfortable talking to another college graduate. He is more tech-savvy and will be uncomfortable with a salesperson who is not at his level.

What about the salespeople currently in dealerships who do not have a college degree or, in some cases, a high school education? Do we fire them or put them out to pasture? Of course not!

The sales manager should look at the educational abilities of each individual salesperson to determine how much additional work may be required to raise that level. The sales manager should encourage dealer salespeople to advance their education and should even provide incentives for them to do it. This could be in the form of subsidizing the education partly or fully, allowing for some time off for classes or providing a bonus on completion of certain courses. If getting a full degree is a viable option for a salesperson, the sales manager should encourage this.

For some salespeople, getting a full degree may prove to be extremely burdensome. An Associate degree could then be a possibility. If even this is not possible, then the sales manager could select certain ag-related or business courses at the local college and encourage the salesperson to attend just these courses. Many colleges allow people who do not have a high school diploma to attend certain courses if they can pass a qualifying test, or they will allow the person to monitor the course.

The sales manager should show some understanding when it comes to education. One example stands out for me. I had been working with a dealership in a small town. One of the salespeople seemed to have a great deal of difficulty when it came to filling out the behavior forms. It turned out that he had never formally learned to read or write. He had taught himself and he secretly felt ashamed that he was not as good as the other salespeople. Despite this handicap, he was still the most productive salesperson in this dealership, regularly outselling the others. He worked harder than the others and had found a way to cope with his deficiencies. I admired him because filling out order forms, a simple task for most people, was a major difficulty for him. He covered it so well that nobody knew that he had any difficulty at all.

When I pointed this out to the dealer principal, he arranged for the salesperson to attend a community college in a neighboring town where he could learn how to read and write properly. This avoided the embarrassment the salesperson would have had attending a local school. The dealer paid for the course. This salesperson was extremely grateful for the considerate confidentiality. He excelled in class and became an even more dedicated salesperson in the dealership. He is still there and nobody in the dealership even knows about this except the owner.

TECHNOLOGY TRAINING

Knowing about technology in a dealership is no longer an option. The salesperson cannot properly function without this knowledge. What should he know?

He should know how to use a computer and become familiar with programs the dealer uses. He should minimally know how to use a database, spreadsheets and the Internet as well as programs that allow him to create quotations. He should be able to access data in the dealer's computer and know how to analyze this data where necessary. If the dealer provides him with a laptop, he should know how to use it and how to keep the data current. In the future, I believe all dealer salespeople will have to be equipped with laptops.

He should be familiar with the technology of the machines he is selling. He does not have to be an expert on this technology but he should understand enough of it to be able to help his customers understand it better. He should learn this technology from a practical, not theoretical, aspect. He should know enough about the technology to be able to compare competitive models.

In areas where this applies, he should have a working knowledge of precision farming. Again, he need not be an expert on this. He should know what it means and have enough knowledge to help his farmer customers understand the applications on their farms. Of course, if he did become an expert in this area, he would stand out in his community and for many miles around.

The salesperson should understand the technologies used by farmers in his area. Again, he need not be an expert on these technologies but he should have enough of a working knowledge to be able to advise the farmer properly. Even though some of these technologies may be beyond the scope of the machinery he sells, he should know about them and be able to advise on them.

You may have noticed that I constantly say that he does not have to be an expert. Does this mean he will have insufficient knowledge? No. So, how much knowledge should he have? Here is a simple test. If you were the farmer customer, how much knowledge would you expect your salesperson to have?

How can the sales manager acquire this knowledge for his salespeople? This is where the manufacturer shines. Make use of every training program you can get. Manufacturers spend vast amounts of money developing these programs to make their dealers more tech-savvy. The sales manager who ignores this gold mine is missing out on tremendous opportunities.

He probably also already has valuable resources in the dealership. Technicians who have learned how to service and repair a machine can pass this knowledge to the salespeople and others in the dealership. Cross-training should always be a source for further education in a dealership. This is the least expensive type of training. Your dealership has already invested in the training of at least one technician. It costs nothing more to have that technician train other technicians or the salespeople.

In one dealership where I suggested this, the parts people jumped on it. They asked to be included in classes the technicians gave to the salespeople. They reasoned that the only time they saw a part, it was in a box. This would give them the opportunity to see the parts where they really belonged. This would help them when discussing parts with their customers.

Of course, when salespeople attend technical workshops, they should come back and be prepared to explain what they had learned to the other salespeople and to others in the dealership.

One danger the sales manager should be aware of: sometimes salespeople learn technicalities but do not see the applications. The sales manager can help. When sending a salesperson to a technical class — or to any sales training class — he should make sure the salesperson takes with him the names of three customers who could benefit from the knowledge he will gain. He should be asked to view the training through the eyes of those customers and come back with solutions for those customers using the training he had just received. He must answer a question on his return. "Why should these customers want to know this?" This puts a more practical aspect to the training. He will learn more efficiently and be more ready to put it into practice sooner.

Every once in a while, the sales manager could bring a competitive machine into the dealership and explain the differences between this model and models that the dealership sells. Salespeople should come into this training with the name of at least one customer who would be interested in the dealer's model. As the sales manager explains the differences, the salespeople should be asking themselves why the customer should choose their model instead of the one being explained. After the demonstration, the sales manager should ask the salespeople to answer this question. Then they should be sent to those customers.

On a regular basis, the sales manager should have one salesperson demonstrate a machine to the other salespeople. This gives them the opportunity to "walk around" a tractor or other piece and to demonstrate the values of that piece. The salesperson should choose one customer to demonstrate to. The other salespeople and the sales manager act as if they are that customer and ask the questions that the customer would ask. The salesperson is told before he begins that he should only demonstrate a feature if he can explain at least one practical application for the farmer he has chosen. The rest of the team judges his performance based on this criterion.

The sales manager can have a competition to see who demonstrates or walks around different pieces the best and award prizes.

Salespeople should be very knowledgeable when it comes to trades. They must be kept up to date on the latest prices that trades are worth. They should look at trades from a profit perspective. The sales manager should make sure that they know the wholesale and retail value of a trade as well as the value to a jockey. They should learn about trades from another perspective, too — where a specific machine is most likely to find a home.

There are many ways a sales manager can develop technological expertise in his salespeople. He can become very creative and innovative in his approach. His manufacturer would be tickled pink if he asked for help. This is exactly what they want him to do.

> ### A REAL EXPERT!
>
> Jim Larson of Haug Implement in Willmar, Minn., is someone I bring up often as an example of a real expert. Jim spent many years in the army working with satellite systems. He joined Haug Implement to help them develop their precision farming business. Jim immediately began learning everything he could about it and became such an expert that farmers came from miles away to learn from him.
>
> You should see his classroom. He has a bank of computers and other high-tech equipment to help him demonstrate to farmers and have them actually touch the technology. He is not only a very knowledgeable person, he is able to share his expertise in language his audience can understand.
>
> He is in great demand. Even Deere calls him for his opinions. Once I was in Idaho. I heard that there was a precision farming expert who was going to be talking to dealers that day in Idaho Falls. Guess who?
>
> Jim is a humble, likeable person with a strong dedication to his field of expertise. I consulted with him often about how to sell it and found him to be like a sponge. His employer, Butch Haug, deserves credit too. Most dealers would not commit to this type of expertise. Butch did it the right way. Is it paying off? I'm not sure, but there is one thing I do know. Butch and Jim are cutting edge people and they will lead the way for others to follow.

SELLING SKILLS

The sales manager should examine the selling skills of his salespeople on a regular basis. He should travel with them and observe them in action. He should note the areas where their skills are deficient or lacking and then find ways to address these.

Some of the selling skills the salesperson should be efficient at are — presentation, asking questions, handling various objections, dealing with price issues, closing, getting commitment, telephone technique, demonstrating equipment, showing value, professionalism and understanding the needs of the customer.

In assessing the selling skills of his salespeople, the sales manager should be as objective as possible. He should not allow his own selling style to cloud his judgement as to the effectiveness of the salesperson. He should remember that different salespeople are more comfortable with their own selling styles. Unless the selling style hurts the sale, the sales manager should try to adapt the correct selling techniques to the style of the salesperson. In selling, there is more than one way to get it done.

Once he has identified the skill that needs developing, he should check to see if the other salespeople have the same problem. If they do, he should find a sales training program that deals specifically with this skill. If this is not a general problem, he should work with the salesperson who has the problem to help him become better in this area.

While selling skill is often the least of the salesperson's problems, the sales manager should regularly check that his salespeople are practicing their skills correctly. Many times salespeople develop bad selling habits because they do not know any better. Having a sales manager check on them is a good way to make sure that they do not continue a bad habit for too long.

BEHAVIORAL SALES TRAINING

Because most salespeople do not fail because they don't know what to do, the sales manager should make sure that they are consistently doing the things they already know how to do. This means getting them to do the things that will generate sales.

Two aspects of this have already been covered earlier in this book. The first is Sales Call Reluctance®. This can destroy a sales career more efficiently than anything else. The second is successful behaviors.

The good sales manager is constantly monitoring the activities of his salespeople. He is not simply looking for sales results. The sales manager who focuses on sales numbers alone will soon have a sales team that also focuses only on numbers. This leads to desperation selling and allows dishonest practices to slip in. He should be monitoring activity as well. If the salespeople perform the right successful behaviors on a consistent basis, the numbers will take care of themselves.

I once sat next to a sales manager on a plane who bragged to me about what a hands-off manager he was. His style of sales management was to tell his salespeople what numbers they had to reach and then allow them to find the ways to get there. There is nothing inherently wrong with this style of management when you have salespeople who are already well-developed and who require very little supervision. I believe this is a good way to manage salespeople who have earned the right to this style of management. I do not believe that all salespeople should be subjected to this style of management simply because it is the style of the sales manager.

He went on to tell me that his salespeople sometimes bent the rules to get the numbers. These were his exact words. "I don't mind the little white lies that they tell the customers as long as they get the job done." This individual fascinated me. He told me he had been a successful salesperson himself and understood how salespeople wanted to be managed. He went on to describe how difficult it was to teach salespeople to close deals and how often he would go with them on a deal and just close it for them because it saved so much time. I wondered how long he would remain a sales manager before he got promoted to some other important position in his company.

I did not contradict him. In fact, after nearly an hour of this, I wished he would just leave me alone. He was enormously proud of the job he was doing. I don't think it even crossed his mind that he was inflicting irreparable damage on the lives of so many people who looked to him for guidance.

I am a strong believer in managing the behaviors of your salespeople. From my perspective, this is the most important job of the sales manager and it shows he genuinely cares about his salespeople.

CONTINUOUS TRAINING

Training should never be treated as events. There has to be some pattern to it, some plan. The good sales manager takes the development of his salespeople seriously. For him, training is not a haphazard tactic based on what the manufacturer is offering this month. It is based on the specific needs of his salespeople and the direction he has decided on.

The good sales manager takes the time to plan the training of his salespeople. He puts a great deal of thought into it. He looks ahead at where he would like them to be and then develops a path to get them there. He does not rely on what is available from the usual sources. Instead, he finds the need and then looks for the best way to address that need. He understands that his salespeople must be continuously developing or else they will be going backwards. He takes tremendous pride in his sales team and wants them to be the best that they can be. He looks for ways to help get them to their best. He's no fool, either. He knows that he is judged on how well his salespeople do and not by the number of memos he sends out or the number of meetings he attends.

Since salespeople develop at different paces, the sales manager should develop a training and education plan for each one he has. He should start with the results — where would he like this salesperson to be one year from now? Then, taking into account the person's present skill level, he should look at how to get him there. He should develop an education and training plan each year for each of his salespeople.

It is not necessary to transform the salesperson in one year. If he can improve each salesperson by just 10% each year, he will have doubled the effectiveness of his sales force within a few years.

So that the education and training program is not one-sided, he should consult with the salesperson in the planning stage. The salesperson should have some guided input into his development and should show some desire to improve. This involvement gives ownership of the training to the salesperson. There should be an agreed time span and the results expected from the training the salesperson will receive. The sales manager should point out to the salesperson that the dealership is investing in him. While this is for the benefit of both, the resources devoted to him are no longer available for anyone else. He should, therefore, make full use of these training resources.

What happens if the salesperson refuses training or refuses to believe that he can benefit from additional training? I have seen some of these salespeople in dealerships. They refuse to admit that they need help. They become defensive about their selling abilities, especially if they have been performing well. They challenge any training on the grounds that the dealer has no confidence in their abilities. In one dealership, I came across a salesperson who had not been to any sales training classes in thirty years with the dealership. He regularly outsold everyone else in the dealership. He viewed all sales training as a waste of time. "You learn on the job," he told me, "and that's all I have ever needed."

He was a paradox. I had no argument with him. Golly, if I were a dealer, I would want 10 of him. He was low-maintenance and he delivered consistently. He did eventually attend one of my sales training classes and demonstrated in it why he was so good at what he did. He contributed a great deal to the class and enhanced the learning of the others. Here was someone who instinctively did the right things. When you added his incredible work ethic, he became almost unbeatable.

I traveled with him and called on customers with him, watching him and learning from him. Did he make mistakes? Sure he made quite a few, but that did not matter. He was effective enough times to cover the mistakes. He even knew when he made mistakes and was not afraid to admit it. After one unsuccessful call, he grinned as we got into his pickup. "I really screwed up on that one, didn't I?" he said. Then it was behind him and he was on to another customer. Another salesperson would have tried to find excuses for the failure. Not him. He messed up. He knew it. He probably would not do the same thing again. So, move on.

What made him come to my sales class? I had pointed out to him that he was an exception. I had asked him how many people he knew who were as good as he was. None. I had asked him how many other salespeople in his dealership could consistently perform as he did. None.

"So, they need help where you don't?"

" Oh, they need a whole lot of help," he told me.

"And you can help them but you won't?"

"I'd help them but they never asked me."

"Yes, they did and you refused."

"When did this happen? I must have been asleep."

"Every time a training opportunity arose that you turned your nose up at, you taught them that training was useless. You showed by your example that you didn't care about them."

He looked about ready to hit me. Then that sheepish grin came back.

"Guess I screwed that one up, didn't I?"

There are not many salespeople like him. Most of the rest who refuse training are simply egos gone mad. The sales manager can help them by insisting that it is not a request but a requirement of the job. He may have an uphill battle on his hands but, if he cares about them, he will fight it. Some sales managers would cut and run, showing that they have given up on a valuable resource. Or they may have that superstar salesperson I met.

COACHING

Every team needs a coach. The sales team is no different. They need someone who cares about them and wants them to become really good. The sales manager fulfills this role.

Sales managers occasionally go out on the road with salespeople, supposedly to coach them. Often, they then miss out on the opportunities to do just that. They spend time in the pickup with the salesperson and chat about hunting or other non-business subjects. The sales manager adds legitimacy and importance to the sales call and then feels good when the sale is made. At the end of the (usually) short day, the sales manager pats the salesperson on the back, tells him how good he is and then feels his coaching for the year has been done.

Sometimes the sales manager goes with the salesperson to show him how to sell. The salesperson is told to observe and the sales manager does the entire selling presentation. On returning to the dealership, the sales manager will usually ask the salesperson if he now knows how to do it and the salesperson will always answer yes. This sales manager feels he has coached by example.

Then there is my friend from the plane. His idea of coaching is to go on a sales call with his salesperson and watch him in action. When he sees him make a mistake, he jumps in and saves the sale. This demonstrates the right way to the salesperson who is expected to learn from it. He loves it when the salesperson has a difficult customer who needs special handling. The sales manager makes the call with the salesperson and shows him how it's done. Unfortunately, the only thing the salesperson learned was: Whenever I have a tough customer, I can call my sales manager. He loves it.

The first question a sales manager should ask himself before going out on a sales call with a salesperson for the purposes of coaching is this: "What would I like to see happen?" There can be several answers to this question but only one right one. The right answer is: "I would like to see my salesperson learn how to sell better."

With this in mind, the sales manager must conduct himself in a way that will allow this learning to happen. He can very easily get distracted and become his own worst enemy in this situation. Instead of jumping in, the sales manager should learn to bite his tongue, to allow the salesperson to make mistakes. After all, most of us learn from the mistakes we make.

After each call, whether it went well or not, the sales manager should debrief the salesperson. Some sales managers make the mistake of approaching this debriefing in a negative manner. "Why," they ask, "do you think the customer did not buy?" This approach usually puts the salesperson on the defensive. He knows that he probably did something wrong and that the sales manager has already identified it. He knows he is in for a lecture. "This is what you should have done…"

Instead, the sales manager should ask the question: "If we had to do that call over again, what would you change?" This same question can be asked whether the call was successful or not. This opens up the salesperson to see things differently, to think the whole process through without defensiveness. The sales manager can guide him but he should be allowed to come to his own conclusions.

All coaching should be approached from this perspective.

If the sales manager wants the salesperson to learn how to sell better as a result of the coaching, then he should allow learning to take place. This applies not only to going on sales calls with salespeople but also to any other coaching opportunities both inside and outside the dealership.

SALES MEETINGS

Most dealership sales meetings I have attended consisted of discussion about product and manufacturer programs. A few allowed salespeople to discuss customers and their needs as they related to the equipment being discussed. There was usually a brief reminder about some used pieces that needed to be moved. Sometimes, there was a discussion about the pricing of certain trades that a salesperson was working on. These are all necessary topics in a sales meeting.

I would like to suggest one additional piece be added in sales meetings — sales training. After each sales meeting, each salesperson should come out knowing more about selling than when he went in. This training need not be lengthy. It could be a short fifteen minute lesson from the sales manager. It could be one of the salespeople delivering a lesson from the field. The sales manager could assign a salesperson a subject that he should be ready to teach to the other salespeople. He could assign a role-play situation to two or more salespeople. The possibilities are endless. No sales meeting should be held without this element of sales training.

The frequency of sales meetings will be determined by the time of year as well as the geography. Multi-store dealerships where the stores are far apart may find it impractical to hold sales meetings every week and expect all salespeople to attend.

How to Manage Salespeople in an Ag Dealership

Wherever possible, there should be a sales meeting once a week, with all salespeople expected to attend. Where this is not possible because of distances, those stores closest to each other should still hold the weekly sales meetings, with the salespeople closest to those stores expected to attend. A full sales meeting for all salespeople from all stores should be held every three to four weeks.

Salespeople need this form of peer contact. Selling is often a lonely business. In dealerships, where salespeople have to travel long distances to get to customers and are often in the field for extended periods, the sales meeting provides an opportunity for them to get connected again. People who have not done this type of selling do not understand the need for this connection.

CHAPTER 16 - LEADING THE SALES TEAM

Whenever more than one salesperson is involved, there exists a sales team. The sales manager needs to lead this team. There are many benefits to a sales team.

1. It provides the connectivity for the individual salespeople.
2. It creates a synergy among the salespeople.
3. It provides a resource pool for ideas.
4. It provides support for the salesperson who experiences periods of flat sales.
5. It allows for competition within the team and competition against other teams.
6. It creates a camaraderie not available to individual salespeople.
7. It allows for the sharing of territories.
8. It becomes a resource pool for labor, allowing people to cover for each other inside the dealership, or when a salesperson goes on vacation.
9. It provides greater security for the dealership. Losing one salesperson does not pose as big a threat.

The sales manager should exploit these advantages so that

every salesperson and the entire dealership benefit. It is more work than managing just one salesperson but the rewards are correspondingly greater.

The sales manager should not overlook the team members inherent in the dealership. The technician can play an important role on a team as can the parts person or the office manager. Everyone in the dealership can be enlisted to be a part of the sales team. Once in a while, the sales department should host a team meeting that includes everyone else in the dealership.

These meetings can consist of updating everyone on what the sales department is doing, and then asking for their support and guidance. One way to garner this support is to make sure that each member of the dealership team is aware of the goals of the sales department and how these goals impact their individual jobs. The technician should be made aware that the sale of a number of certain tractors, for example, affects how much service work will become available to him. He should also be shown how he could influence the purchase of wholegoods by the quality of service he performs. He should also be shown how poor service work negatively affects the sale of wholegoods. Re-work, for example, not only hurts the service department, it erodes customer confidence in the dealership and can prevent future sales.

In many dealerships, there is a lack of cooperation between departments. Parts people often complain about the lack of patience from the service technicians while the technicians cannot understand why the parts people cannot get them the right parts on time. Both departments complain about salespeople who, without first consulting them, regularly make promises to customers that involve their departments. Office personnel have an on-going feud with salespeople over paperwork. All of this does not create an atmosphere of teamwork. While many dealerships talk a good game about the teamwork they have, the truth is that there is very little of it.

This is particularly true of larger dealerships and multi-store operations. Smaller dealerships almost force teamwork because of the fewer number of employees. In one two-store operation, the owners decided to unite the stores and had jackets made for all the employees. On the backs of the jackets, in beautiful bold letters, were the names of both stores. The employees in one of the stores refused to wear the jackets because their store name did not appear first.

Salespeople in multi-store operations can be vicious when it comes to this lack of teamwork. Concerned about their commissions, they "hide" good trades from salespeople in the other stores so that only they will have the opportunity to sell them. I have even seen salespeople from different stores of the same group cutting prices on each other so that the customer will buy from one store and not the other. I have seen sales managers encourage this!

The sales manager should control this type of behavior, since it is not in the best interests of the dealership or of a cohesive sales team. He should accept responsibility for developing teamwork not only among the salespeople but also in the entire dealership. While he may not be able to control the people in other departments, he can at least make it easier for them to cooperate with his salespeople.

Whenever I do teamwork workshops as part of the Successful Dealer Behaviors Program in dealerships, I always ask a few simple questions. First, I will outline a situation, such as:

> *The salesperson promises a customer that a seemingly minor part will be replaced immediately if the customer brings the equipment in. He does not tell the service department and does not check with the parts department to make sure this part is available. The*

customer arrives at the dealership and finds that the shop is too busy to do the repair immediately and, in any case, the part has to be ordered. The service manager tries his best to satisfy the customer while cursing the salesperson under his breath.

Most technicians, service managers and parts people will nod their heads knowingly at this example. Someone will inevitably pipe up, "You know our salespeople, don't you!"
Here are the questions:

- Why do you think the salesperson did it?
- Do you think it was done deliberately to make you mad?
- How many of you would like to have happy customers?
- How many of you would go out of your way to have happy customers?
- Was the salesperson perhaps doing it for the same reason?

The point I make is that the intention is always good. When a technician gets mad because a part is not available, the reason is because he does not want the customer to wait any longer than is necessary for the repair to be completed. Everyone in the dealership has the right intention. How they go about it is what causes the problem. When everyone understands that they all want the same thing, and that getting that same thing is possible, they become a bit more considerate of others in the dealership and also a bit more forgiving when others slip up occasionally.

Whenever there is friction between the sales department and other departments, I always blame the sales department. Why? They have the ability to change the situation. They have been trained to sell and they should use this training to sell the other departments on getting along with them and working with them for the benefit of their customers. They forget that the other departments are their customers, too. Whenever salespeople ignore this ability to make a change in the relationship, they show a disregard for all customers and a lack of selling competence.

By involving the other dealership personnel in the sales effort, the sales manager can generate a better team spirit in the entire dealership. One dealer I know does this admirably. Whenever any salesperson makes a big sale, the dealer rings a bell in the dealership, telling everyone what's happened. The salesperson immediately appears with a bag of donuts or some other treat to share with everyone in the dealership. This is his way of thanking them for making the sale possible.

THE SALES TEAM

The sales team should, by definition, be a unit. Each person on the team should be an essential part of the unit. The sales manager should encourage this unity and should provide rules for the team. There should be consequences for breaking the rules as well as rewards when the team does well.

The sales manager should set individual as well as team targets. If the team reaches its targets, every member of the team should be rewarded. If the team target is not met, then there is no team reward even if some individuals met their personal targets. The team targets should be set in cooperation with the members of the team. Although the sales manager is the leader, he should allow for member contributions to the setting of goals and team behaviors.

Once the team goals have been set, the sales manager should elicit suggestions from the team members as to how these objections can be met. Here are some questions he can ask to stimulate creativity.

MANAGING IRON SALESPEOPLE

1. What do we need to do beyond what we are already doing to reach our team targets?
2. What must we do differently to get us there faster?
3. What will be my contribution to this effort?
4. How can we enlist the support of other personnel in the dealership to get us there faster?

MOTIVATING THE TEAM

It is a human trait to want to belong. If a sales team is an attractive unit, then just belonging to it is already a reward. However, this should not be the only reward. The sales manager should provide opportunities for the salespeople to be rewarded for team efforts. This could take the form of bonuses if the team achieves its targets or simply a pat on the back for smaller achievements. Whatever he does, the sales manager should acknowledge team efforts. He should devise a system that rewards for behaviors he would like to see more of.

He wants to keep the team spirit reasonably high throughout the year, especially during slow times.

One way to do this is to disclose his business plans for the department and how he sees the team accomplishing these plans. Financial disclosure is important. He should be able to show them, in graphic form, what his vision for the coming year is. Then, each month, he should show them how they are progressing towards this target.

Sales managers often make the mistake of selling their salespeople a load of hogwash. When the sales team is not performing as well as they should and they are not achieving their objectives, he tells them that they deserve a reward for effort anyway. He covers the flaws with flowery language so that they will feel good about themselves. This is a delusion. Salespeople are not fools. They know when they have not done as well as they should. Glossing over it makes the sales manager look like a wimp and a liar. Instead of doing this, the sales manager should assertively tell them that they did not do what they should have done and this is why the target had not been reached. He can then tell them that more will have to be done to catch up and ask them for suggestions on what they can do to get their plan on track again.

Team outings, especially to celebrate a victory, can do a great deal to lift team spirits. If the salespeople play golf, a golf outing can be a prized reward. Even a celebration lunch at a local restaurant can be worthwhile. If a technician or someone in the dealership contributed to the reason for celebration, take that person along.

Provide competitions within the team. For example, if a particular competitor often outsells the salespeople, have a contest to see who can come up with the best solution to this problem. Have everyone contribute a dollar and give the money to the one who gets voted as having the most innovative or practical solution.

In multi-store operations, have one store's sales team compete with another store's. Instead of making the competition to see who can make the most sales, let them see how many other-color customers they can convert within the next month or how many profiles they can collect.

Here's an idea I have promoted to dealerships that has found avid acceptance. Whenever you give a cash reward, withhold part of it. This part goes into a Christmas Fund for the salesperson. If, for example, the reward is $50, hold $25 and only give $25. The held money goes into that salesperson's Christmas Fund and accumulates interest. The salesperson receives this fund one week before Christmas. I like this idea for several reasons.

MANAGING IRON SALESPEOPLE

One is because the salesperson gets rewarded twice. Another is because I don't know anyone who would refuse extra cash a week before Christmas.

If the sales manager is inventive enough, he can come up with a host of ideas to keep his salespeople motivated and on-track throughout the year.

FACTS ABOUT LEADERSHIP

Leadership is not about getting the job done. Leadership is getting things done through others.

You need your employees more than they need you.

You get paid for what they do, not for what you do.

Your reason for being there is to do everything in your power to help your employees to be as successful as they can be.

You succeed only when they succeed.

BE A LEADER
Develop tactics from your customer's point of view.
Communicate persuasively. State your vision simply and repeatedly.
Behave with integrity. Employees pay more attention to what you do than what you say.
Respect others.
Manage assertively and consistently.

"In this world there are leaders and there are followers. There is neither shame nor glory in being one or the other. However, there is deceit attached to those who claim to be leaders and then fail to fulfill their roles as leaders."
Frank Lee in a speech to managers

CHAPTER 17 - SALESPERSON ACCOUNTABILITY

One of the more important jobs of the sales manager is to keep the salespeople accountable for what they do. This is not an easy task, since salespeople would rather not be accountable and can be very creative in how they dodge it. What should they primarily be accountable for?

Since time is their biggest asset, then time is what they should be accountable for. This is not to say that the sales manager should not hold them accountable for achieving targets and performing successful behaviors. However, the accountability I will describe in this chapter is often overlooked in dealerships. In fact, farm equipment dealerships are the only sales-driven businesses I have ever worked with where the salespeople are *not* held accountable for their time.

Call reports do not exist in most dealerships. As for planning, that's a foreign subject. To keep salespeople accountable for their time, the sales manager must know two things — what they plan to do and what they did.

PLANNING SHEETS

The first requires that the salesperson should plan his time. This means developing ahead of time how he plans to spend his week. Each salesperson should be required to provide the sales manager with a weekly plan of activities. The sales manager should create his own planning form. An example is given on page 170. Each salesperson should hand a copy of this weekly plan to the sales manager each Monday morning. The sales manager should make a copy available to the office personnel so that they are also aware of where each salesperson will be during the week. The weekly plan should list all planned activities such as customer calls, phone calls and meetings.

Salespeople in dealerships seem to hate this activity. I remember one hot-shot salesperson who told his manager, "I don't care. You can fire me, but I will not tell anyone where I'm going!" Of course, he was not fired because he was a big producer and none of the other salespeople completed weekly planning sheets, either.

The sales manager should examine the planning sheets. There is no point in collecting them if he will not. He should look for gaps so that he can help them plan better. Some sales managers seem to think that this is a way to keep track of their salespeople. Yes, but it is far more than that. The reason for the planning sheet is to get salespeople into the habit of planning their activities so that they are not simply reacting to things that happen during the day. They become more proactive and start to value their time more.

Whenever I introduce planning into the lives of dealer salespeople, at least one person will tell me that I don't understand the business. "By nine, the plan is already in the toilet!" In other words, it does not make sense to plan. They always tell me how busy they are. And I believe them — to a point. I have been with enough dealer salespeople to know that they have to get a lot accomplished in a day. I also know that they waste a tremendous amount of time and a plan, any plan, would save them time. Besides, as I remind them, planning is for busy people. If you're not busy, what do you have to plan? Planning allows busy people to do more.

When the sales manager first introduces the planning sheet, he will find salespeople handing in incomplete sheets. This is an indication that they did not think through their week properly. It could also be an indication that they simply are not as busy as they would like him to believe. Instead of having an argument over how much time the salesperson has not planned for, the sales manager should simply fill in the time for him.

"It looks like you have nothing happening on Wednesday, so I would like you to take an hour and make some cold calls on the phone."

The salesperson now has one of two responses. He can say that he actually will be busy on Wednesday and invent an activity or he will have to make the cold calls. If he claims an activity that is not on the planning sheet, the sales manager should call him on it.

"Then why didn't you put it into your plan? Were you faking it when you drew up your plan or are you faking it now?"

The sales manager only has to do this twice and he will start to see those planning sheets fill up. Now he has to look for padding. This is when a salesperson puts in a fake activity simply to fill space on the planning sheet.

One of the most effective ways to put an end to padding is to select one of the activities on the sheet and tell the salesperson that he will accompany him on that visit. For example, "I see you are planning to visit Farmer Jones on Thursday. I'd like to go on that call with you."

If the activity is fake, the salesperson can admit it and

make a real appointment in a hurry. Or he can compound the lie by telling the sales manager later in the week that the appointment was canceled. In any case, the point had been made. The salesperson will not know which activity the sales manager will decide to do with him and he may start to put activities that are more genuine on his planning sheet.

The exercise is not designed to belittle or punish salespeople. It is designed to help them become the best they can be. A sales manager who ignores this cannot claim to genuinely care about his salespeople.

After a short while, the salespeople will develop the habit of planning their days and weeks properly. Although the sales manager will lead them kicking and screaming to it, they will remember him and thank him for it. He will have helped them to become salespeople who are more professional.

PLANNING SHEET EXAMPLE

Day	Apps	To Call	Calling me	To Do
Monday				
Tuesday				
Wed				
Thursday				
Friday				
Saturday				

CALL REPORTS

After each sales call, a record should be made as to what happened during the sales call and what action must follow. This is another activity most dealer salespeople resist. They claim that they have it "up here", pointing to their brains. Yet, when tested on their memories of things that occurred that day, they are often wrong about details. Rather than leaving it to a sometimes imperfect memory, they should commit it to a written record. Besides, they forget that nobody else has it "up here" and cannot read their minds.

The sales manager should insist on proper sales call reports. Each salesperson should be equipped with a number of report forms and be required to turn these in once a week. The sales manager should examine each call report to familiarize himself with their activities and to check that the follow-through actions are not slipping through the cracks. He should design his own call reports based on the information he needs to properly manage his salespeople. An example is shown on page 172. He should make this as simple as possible without sacrificing important information.

He should compare the call reports to the planning sheets to make sure that activities planned for have been done. This will also help him detect any padding of the planning sheet.

He should be on the lookout for "awning calls" that salespeople have become notorious for. That's when a salesperson claims to have called on a customer. Rather than outright lie about not making the call, the salesperson will arrive at the door of the customer and stand under the awning for a few seconds before leaving. He can now legitimately claim that he made the call even though he shows nothing for it.

By asking salespeople about specific calls they made and getting details, the sales manager will learn how to detect "awning calls." After just a little experience, most sales managers are able to spot them. The sales manager should never allow the salesperson to get away with any type of fake reporting. This makes a mockery of the system and teaches the salesperson that he can fool the sales manager. This does not help the career of the salesperson or the business of the dealership.

When the sales manager makes the planning sheets and the call reports non-negotiable behaviors, he has taken a huge step towards making the salespeople accountable for their time. In the end, it is not only the sales manager who benefits. The salespeople ultimately become accountable to the people who really matter — themselves.

EXAMPLE OF A CALL REPORT

Customer	Reason for call	Result of call	Follow up Action	Dept. to notify

CHAPTER 18 - EMPOWERING THE SALESPERSON

Throughout this book, I have talked about managing salespeople, from targets to activities. It may seem that I do not believe salespeople can manage themselves. This is not true. I have met a number of salespeople who do an excellent job of managing their time and their careers. I have just not met that many in dealerships. They exist. I have just not had the pleasure of meeting too many of them.

MICRO-MANAGEMENT

This does not mean that I advocate micro-managing them forever. I believe that, in the early stages of professional sales management in dealerships, micro-management of salespeople is essential. However, I am against micro-management forever. If the time of the sales manager is taken up with micro-managing salespeople who will never be able to take charge of their own careers, then the sales manager would do well to let them go early and save himself, and them, a lot of headaches.

The truth is that many salespeople only reach stardom after they have acquired the habits of success. There is never a dispute among salespeople as to what these habits are or whether they should acquire them. They agree that they will be successful if they perform the right successful behaviors as a matter of habit. However, agreement does not always translate into sales. This is where the good sales manager comes in. He will help the salesperson develop these habits by using micro-management to micro-manage behaviors.

My preference is for salespeople to come off of micro-management as quickly as possible. This will only be possible when they earn the right to come off it. There should be predetermined time constraints. A salesperson who never comes off micro-management should be let go. The cost in management time is simply not worth the investment.

How does a salesperson earn the right? When he demonstrates by his behavior that he is capable of managing his own career, when he does what he says without supervision, when he shows a pattern of such behavior, and when the sales manager can see demonstrable proof that he is now entitled to be empowered.

WHAT AND HOW MUCH AUTHORITY?

Salespeople should quickly learn how to trade like business people. Once they have, the sales manager should set parameters and allow them to operate within those parameters - not so narrow as to stifle the authority but not broad enough to cost the dealership.

Once the salesperson has demonstrated his ability to

properly work his territory, the sales manager should ease off and allow him to make decisions in his territory. Again, he should be given very clear parameters and then left alone.

Salespeople could be involved in the dealership's wholegoods advertising. When they demonstrate their abilities in this area, the sales manager can safely leave certain advertising to them.

When salespeople show that they regard used equipment as a source of income and demonstrate that they can move it without supervision, they should be given some leeway in doing this.

If a new salesperson joins the team and shares a territory, the experienced salesperson with good successful behaviors could take the new salesperson under his wing and help in his education and training. This does not mean that the sales manager abdicates his responsibility for training new salespeople. It means that the experienced salespeople can help in the training. Whenever this occurs, the experienced salesperson should get a piece of the action. He could get an overriding commission on all sales in his territory made by the new salesperson or he could get a bonus for his efforts.

While the sales manager never gives up authority or responsibility, he should delegate some of his authority to his better salespeople. This allows them to feel more valuable and prepares them to eventually take over the role of the sales manager. A good sales manager is always training someone to take over his job. In a smaller dealership, the actual promotion may not occur easily, but the possibility should always be there. The good sales manager is never concerned about losing his job to someone he has trained. He knows that developing people to become better than he is a much sought-after trait. The sales manager who is able to do this will never be out of work. He attracts good people because he develops a reputation for improving them and furthering their careers.

KNOW YOUR SALESPEOPLE

For the sales manager to properly develop his replacement, he should get to know his salespeople on a very personal level. He should know the strengths and weaknesses of each and be constantly increasing the strengths while fixing the weaknesses.

He should understand their personal goals as well as their career goals. He must know what turns them on and find ways to help them achieve those personal goals. He should know their families and what the job means to their families.

This does not make him a close family friend. There should always be that little bit of distance. However, he can be a friend and counselor for the salesperson. Taking a genuine interest in the lives of his salespeople will allow him to do this. Salespeople generally look up to their sales manager and rely on them for career guidance. The best sales manager is usually described as someone who cares about me and goes to bat for me. Even as the sales manager cares and goes to bat for his salespeople, he should always strive to maintain their respect.

CHAPTER 19 - EVALUATING PERFORMANCE

The best way to evaluate the performance of a salesperson is to start with observable, objective measures. How will you know that your salesperson is improving? Before you can answer that question, you must first answer some other questions.

1. What does improvement mean to you?
2. Are you able to measure it?
3. What will you measure?

To some sales managers, improvement in salespeople simply means that they are making more sales this year than they did last year. That is enough to satisfy them. They can objectively measure this and they only have one thing to measure.

In dealerships, things get a little more complicated. More sales do not necessarily mean improvement. The additional sales can result from a drastic change in the economy or in the price of one commodity. Additional sales do not always translate into additional profits if there were some bad deals along the way. Volume is a deceptive thing in the dealership. I have met some dealers who produce huge volumes and who are loved by their manufacturers. However, their margins are razor-thin and their absorption factor is too low. They do not make enough money and they do not have enough aftermarket business despite their high volumes. They may be outselling their capacity to service what they sell. Salespeople who contribute to this situation cannot be said to be improving.

WHY MEASURE?

Why measure at all? Isn't this more hard work?

The good sales manager is always checking to make sure that he is moving himself, his salespeople and the dealership in the right direction. He does not rely on feelings. Rather, he uses the right tools to guide him. He knows that, in any business, one can easily become distracted by daily activities that cloud the issue of improvement. Besides, he started out with a business plan in mind and wants to know how he is progressing towards that plan.

His salespeople also want to know that he is monitoring their progress. Besides giving them the comforting feeling that someone cares enough about them to measure them, it has important business applications. The owners of the dealership are measuring the sales manager. They have very definite ideas of what constitutes successful sales management. He had better find out what those ideas are so that he can demonstrate that he is meeting their objectives. By having a clear measuring device, he also knows when he is not making progress and can take the right corrective action early.

WHAT TO MEASURE

There are certain obvious things to measure such as sales volume and number of units sold. Then there are some not so obvious.

As a matter of good business, each salesperson should be evaluated on the following:

1. Dollar volume on a day-by-day basis.
2. Number of units sold versus projected numbers.
3. Used inventory build-up.
4. Margins.
5. Numbers of sales.
6. Numbers of customers in varying categories.

These will tell him if his salespeople are trading correctly. In evaluating their performance of successful behaviors and their effectiveness, he should also monitor and measure the following:

1. Percentage of territory being covered as compared to desired coverage.
2. Number of other-color conversions.
3. Number of proposals being generated.
4. Number of closings in relationship to the number of proposals.
5. Close ratios.
6. Number of new prospects in the pipeline.
7. Number and quality of profiles collected, updated and analyzed.
8. Profit per sale.
9. Number of on-farm demonstrations.

Most of the above can be tracked using software that is

readily available. Some manufacturers build tracking into their proprietary software that the dealer uses anyway. Adding a few additional items should not present a major problem.

MONTHLY REVIEWS

The sales manager should review the above data with the salespeople each month at one of the sales meetings. All the data should be made available to them. They should compare where they are in relation to where they should be according to the targets they had set. If they are behind target, the sales manager should draw up an immediate plan of action to remedy the situation. The salespeople should be involved in drawing up this plan of action since they will be putting it into practice.

If they are ahead of target, the sales manager should use this momentum to set higher targets if he can see a pattern of momentum. (Two months of beating the targets would convince me that there was a pattern.) Momentum is a tremendous sales tool to set sales records. The sales manager should not be afraid to use it. Salespeople can feel the momentum and this generates excitement. The sales manager can lose this excitement if he does not build on it.

SALESPERSON REVIEWS

Most dealerships conduct annual reviews of all employees for the purposes of determining how the employee has progressed over the past year and to set targets for the following year. They also use this review to set a pay scale for the following year. I think this is a mistake. The annual review should not discuss pay. This should be a separate meeting.

The sales manager should conduct regular reviews with each salesperson. I recommend at least twice a year. The purpose of this review is not to discuss pay issues but to evaluate the performance of the salesperson and to agree on performance improvements.

This review should be taken seriously by both the sales manager and the salesperson. It should not be a hurried affair with many interruptions. The review meeting should not be interrupted except for absolute emergencies. A minimum time for the review should be set and an agenda provided to the salesperson ahead of time. The salesperson should have an opportunity to add items to this agenda. All reviews should be properly documented in the employee files.

At the review, the sales manager should deal with issues and not personalities. It's a time to discuss the past performance of the salesperson in terms of targets that were met or missed. He should examine with the salesperson the reasons why targets were not met and determine the best course of action for dealing with them. If further training is required, he should agree with the salesperson as to what training he will undergo, when, and with what expected results. The sales manager should avoid finger-pointing, especially on something that may have occurred several months ago. If performance is not up to scratch, there is no point in bringing up specific examples of past mistakes unless these can help the salesperson understand the reasons for his lack of performance.

Make the whole review process positive so the salesperson feels that the reason for the review is to help him improve. The sales manager should avoid all outbursts of temper and keep emotion out of the review. If the salesperson is hostile to criticism, the review should be cut short and the salesperson told to come back for a further review when he is more amenable to a reasonable discussion. If any actions are agreed to, these should be documented and the salesperson should sign his agreement. There should be a definite time for these actions to occur. The next review meeting should be set to coincide with this time period.

If the sales manager conducts the review in a positive, helpful manner, it can be a useful tool in the development of the salesperson. If the sales manager is not sure how to conduct a review, he should get outside help before doing it. Too many reviews end up with nothing positive being achieved because the sales manager did not have any clear ideas about the review and did not know what should result from it.

Since reviews are necessary and important, the sales manager should acquaint himself with the laws of the state where he conducts business as well as proper review procedures. I am no expert on employee reviews. The above should serve as a guideline only. The sales manager should find the proper instructions on employee reviews.

CHAPTER 20 - STRATEGIC SALES PLANNING

If the sales manager would like to increase the business of the dealership, there are only three sources of new business

1. Increase sales to existing customers
2. Find new customers
3. Create new markets

INCREASING EXISTING CUSTOMER SALES

Several years ago, I asked a dealer how many customers made up eighty percent of his business. I was surprised to learn that it was only fifteen. How many total customers did he have? According to his computer database, hundreds.

My second surprise came when I discovered that his top customers did not give him all of their business. They tended to spread their business out over a few dealers. I asked him why they did this. He felt it was because they were not comfortable giving one dealer all of their business. I have since asked several dealer salespeople the same question and have gotten several variations on the same answer.

Not satisfied, I started asking farmers the same question. They were more forthright. It seemed they were not altogether satisfied with their main dealer. One reason they gave him the bulk of their business, it seemed, was because he was the best of a bad bunch. Other reasons they gave were that the dealer did not always have everything they needed and that they could bargain better if the dealer knew he was not getting all of their business.

I began to play "what if?" games with myself. What if the dealer wanted to get all of the business from its top customers? What would the dealer have to do to make the customer want to give him all of the business? What if this was impossible? Can the dealer at least close the gap somewhat? If he wanted to, what would he need to do?

I confess I did not have all the answers so I continued asking dealers and their customers. The result of all this became the Most Valued Customer/Teamwork Workshop that I developed and delivered to several dealerships around the country. The premise of the first part of this workshop is that the dealer can close the gap between what the customer spends with him and what he spends in total, but he has to plan for it to happen. We already knew it would not happen by accident. We also knew that the dealer was not fulfilling all of the needs of the customer.

Because the customer, by his own admission, regarded the entire dealership as his supplier, the entire dealership needed to be willing to do additional things to make the customer willing to spend more money with the dealership. Since this is not something that can be changed overnight, the salespeople had to develop a strategic sales plan on how to close this gap.

Working in teams led by a salesperson, everyone in the dealership becomes involved in developing this strategic sales plan. This is a very practical workshop. Each salesperson comes in armed with detailed information about a specific customer. This customer becomes the focus of each team. I usually try to get a good mix - technicians, parts people, office personnel, and a salesperson on each team. We start out by determining the full potential value of the customer. We already know how much this customer is spending in the dealership on wholegoods, parts and service. We then determine what the gap is and by what percentage we would like to close that gap in the next 12 months.

Then, working in teams, they develop a detailed strategic sales plan that will allow them to close that gap by the desired percentage. By the end of the first day of this workshop, they have a completed sales plan that accounts for all sales to this customer. They will also have learned the value of the profile and how to use it.

The sales manager should do this exercise with his salespeople. Rather than to rely on chance, he should teach them how to develop strategic sales plans. It is always a good idea to involve the other departments in this strategic planning session. They bring a different perspective and a great deal of good ideas to the table. The sales manager should select only the top customers for this exercise. He should not be swayed by the salesperson who says that the customer is already buying everything from the dealership. He should check it out and confirm this for himself. If true, then select a different customer. I have been amazed at how little some salespeople knew about their supposedly top customers.

ACQUIRING NEW MOST VALUED CUSTOMERS

With the shrinking farmer customer base, it becomes increasingly urgent for dealers to acquire additional top-dollar customers. Other dealerships close up, but getting their best customers is not an automatic process. The only other sources for such customers are your remaining competitors and they are not likely to hand their top customers over to anyone.

The sales manager should teach his salespeople how to strategically acquire such new customers. Let me tell you how I have gotten dealers to acquire new, high-value customers.

In the second part of the Most Valued Customer/Teamwork Workshop, we concentrate on the acquisition of new Most Valued Customers. The premise of this part of the workshop is that, if each salesperson can acquire just one new Most Valued Customer each year, he will destroy the competition and strengthen the dealership. If each salesperson plans to acquire three each year and only succeeds in getting one, the dealership is still way ahead of the game.

Again, working in teams, they develop a strategic sales plan to acquire a specific new high-value customer. Each salesperson comes into this workshop armed with the name of a customer he would like to acquire. We agree that it is highly unlikely that the customer will willingly come into the dealership and we agree that it is unlikely that the customer will spend all of his money with the dealership immediately. Based on what we collectively know about this prospect, we estimate his worth as a customer for wholegoods, parts and service. We examine what business, if any, he already does with the dealership. We then set a target for how much of his business we can reasonably expect to take away from the competition in the following 12 months.

The teams then develop a strategic sales acquisition plan to make it happen. They examine things that they currently do that could be of interest to the new customer and things that they could collectively do to acquire him piecemeal. I teach them a technique I call "putting your arms around" that will bring even the most difficult prospect into the dealership. I also teach them about positioning themselves to make the new customer's visits to the dealership more rewarding.

By the end of this day, the salespeople have a completed strategic sales plan to acquire this new customer in the next 12 months.

One of the big disappointments of mine in dealerships came with this program. I saw technicians and setup people show much more enthusiasm and interest in acquiring new customers than the salespeople. In some dealerships, the salespeople appeared disconcerted by all of this. It was almost as if they wished they did not have to do any work to acquire additional customers even though they said they wanted to. This was not always the case. There were many salespeople who took this and ran with it and who ended up making many more sales.

I will never forget one salesperson who sat very quietly in the workshop. I was not worried because I could see he was absorbing the material. He seemed a little lost but he was like a sponge. I could almost hear the whooshing sound as the material got drawn into him. After the workshop, he spoke to me. This was the first real sales training he had received. He told me that it had opened his eyes to doing business differently and that he could apply what he had just learned immediately. He told me of a customer he had in mind and outlined the steps he was going to take. I liked him.

It can be done. What is needed is a leader who cares about the development of his salespeople. What is needed is a good sales manager who will push the envelope. The sales manager can enlist the entire dealership to help or he can simply lead his sales team to think strategically about acquiring new customers.

Whichever way he does it, he can make a real difference simply by trying.

> ### "I JUST WITNESSED A MIRACLE!"
>
> Bob Hilleque, a top trainer from John Deere, sat in on one of my ***Most Valued Customer/Teamwork*** workshops. At the end, he told me that he had witnessed a minor miracle.
> "In all of my 29 years with Deere," he told me, "I have never seen a technician develop a sales plan."
> "How many dealer salespeople have you seen do it?" I asked.
> He shook his head and smiled.

DEVELOPING NEW MARKETS

Today, there are many non-agricultural uses for agriculturally-related machinery. If the dealership is not already involved in these emerging markets, this can be an excellent opportunity for the sales manager. If they are already in these markets, he should find ways to expand them.

He should be creative and encourage creativity in his salespeople. If the new markets in his area are lucrative enough, he should consider hiring a salesperson who would specialize in the new markets.

He should also look at expanding existing markets. For example, if the dealership already bids on certain government contracts, he should look at bidding on other contracts that may at first appear to be outside of his realm. He should explore and ask questions.

Whether he wants to develop a new market or expand an existing one, he should enlist his sales team to plan a strategic assault. Rather than picking up pieces of new business at random, this should be a concerted effort, well planned and executed.

If he is not sure how to develop such strategic plans, there are several training programs that will teach him how to do it. Most would be theoretical because they are not specific for his industry, but this is one case where even a theoretical workshop can help.

USED EQUIPMENT

The sales manager should read the chapter on used equipment in my book, *"P.A.S.S. C.A.L.F. - 8 Behaviors of Sales Success in an Agricultural Dealership"*.

Used equipment in dealerships often tends to be ignored until the owner sees all of his money lying outside and starts to rant and rave. Then panic selling sets in. The salespeople are told to move the stuff, or else! This should not be the case.

Used equipment is an essential part of a dealership's business. Without it, new equipment would be harder to move. The sales manager should regard it in this light and develop a strategic position on moving used equipment. It should never be allowed to accumulate. There should be a consistent strategy in place that allows for the sale of used equipment as an on-going business.

The sales manager should teach the salespeople how to always be on the lookout for buyers for the used equipment they trade in. One dealer I know does not have this problem. The way he sells new equipment is first to look at the trade he is likely to have to take. He finds a home for this trade before he even approaches the prospect. Many times, he will have sold several used pieces before he even talks to the customer about the new equipment. And he makes money with each trade. And he is not stuck with useless used equipment. He thinks the entire sale through strategically and then puts his plan into action.

The sales manager may never get the salespeople to this

dealer's level but he could get them moving in the right direction.

CHAPTER 21 - CREATING SUPERSTAR SALESPEOPLE

This chapter is a summary of some of what has gone before. If the sales manager wants to acquire and develop superstar salespeople, here is what he will have to do:

1. Start right by hiring the right people.
2. Genuinely care about the salespeople.
3. Provide meaningful sales training.
4. Teach salespeople the right disciplines and work ethic.
5. Get the new salesperson started quickly. Remember the value of early performance.
6. Continuously educate the salespeople, especially on technology.
7. Coach them constantly.
8. Coach for a successor sales manager.
9. Motivate them consistently.
10. Take the time to understand them.
11. Use momentum to set sales records.
12. Involve the entire dealership.
13. Set realistic targets, both dollar targets and behavioral

targets.
14. Make the salespeople accountable for reaching the targets.
15. Make the salespeople accountable for their time.
16. Develop proper sales processes.
17. Develop a strong team.
18. Train the salespeople to think strategically.
19. Develop new markets.
20. Measure and evaluate.
21. Review salespeople often.
22. When they are ready, empower them.

23. Develop and manage successful behaviors!

If the sales manager does all of the above, he will stand an excellent chance of creating a team of sales superstars.

CHAPTER 22 - 8 SUCCESSFUL BEHAVIORS FOR SALES MANAGERS

I am ending this book with some successful behaviors for the sales manager. After all, if successful behaviors are good for salespeople, they should be good for the sales manager too.

Here are eight successful behaviors that I believe all sales managers should practice.

1. Plan your days.

2. Educate yourself. The sales manager should set aside learning time on how to become a better sales manager.

3. Create a healthy environment in the dealership that encourages achievement. This is not a one-time event but an on-going effort. Create excitement. Lose the excuses.

4. Develop a competitive sales team. Constantly find ways to challenge them.

MANAGING IRON SALESPEOPLE

5. Develop proper sales processes. Continue to develop, change or improve the processes.

6. Take the time to really know your salespeople. This includes their families.

7. Travel with each salesperson at least once every week.

8. Impart some sales training every week.

CONCLUSION

Does it still look as if sales management in a dealership is a part-time job?

There is far more to sales management than most dealers realize. This is why I do not foresee any major changes in this area for a while yet. Dealers will continue to claim that they cannot afford a full-time sales manager. Perhaps this book will convince them that a professional sales manager can earn far more than he costs.

I know that most dealers will still wait. For them, this will still be a Seinfeld episode. However, they will eventually realize two things.

1. They are already paying for a sales manager in the form of lost sales and lost opportunities.

2. To grow their businesses strategically, they may not have a choice.

    There is a definite need for a full-time sales manager in a dealership. Those dealers who realize this and do something about it now are the ones most likely to survive and prosper in the new millennium.

ABOUT THE AUTHOR

Frank Lee has taught thousands of people the value of "Beyond FAB" selling.

Other salespeople, and such notable authors as George W. Dudley, have hailed Frank as a sales superstar, a master salesperson, and a great sales manager. However, Frank will tell you his skills are no more than average. Certainly, he knows and understands basic selling strategies. He will admit to many years of diverse selling experiences. He will even confess to having been extremely successful as a salesperson and sales manager.

What he attributes his selling successes to is something of a surprise. It is not, as he says, due to his "dazzling charm, wit and intelligence." Rather, it is something far more basic and achievable. Frank credits his successful selling career to practicing successful behaviors on a consistent daily basis. These successful behaviors have helped him create and run businesses in seven countries. They have catapulted him from a start-up operation to one of the largest sellers of the Fear-Free Prospecting and Self-Promotion Workshop® in the world—in less than three years.

These behaviors are not only simple, they are achievable by any dedicated salesperson.

His books are a combination of his years of experience using successful behaviors, his experience traveling with many agricultural equipment salespeople, working with hundreds of dealerships, and numerous workshops he has conducted in eleven countries.

Today, with offices in Texas and Singapore, Frank Lee continues to sell in huge quantities and to teach salespeople in many industries - especially the Ag industry - how to make "successful behaviors" work for them, too.

He lives in Flower Mound, Texas but regularly travels all over the United States and overseas. He is married and has two children and two dogs, all of whom he is extremely proud.

P.A.S.S. C.A.L.F. - 8 BEHAVIORS OF SALES SUCCESS IN AN AGRICULTURAL DEALERSHIP

P.A.S.S. C.A.L.F. deals with sales issues that confront agricultural equipment salespeople every day of their lives. This is not a book for the theorist; nor is it a comprehensive sales skills workbook.

It explains sales success in terms of successful behaviors and shows salespeople how to perform these successful behaviors consistently to achieve world class results.

The behaviors come straight from the field. The author currently teaches them to agricultural salespeople all over the United States. They form the basis of a behavioral sales workshop delivered to dealers all over North America.

P.A.S.S. C.A.L.F. is not just for agricultural salespeople. These behaviors apply to salespeople in most industries. They are currently part of the sales training of one of the largest banking conglomerates in the United States.

Now available in audio book format so that dealer salespeople can listen to it in their pickups. Read by Bob Gee, the entire book is contained on 2 audio cassettes.

We recommend dealers buy both the book and the audio cassettes for maximum use by their salespeople.

TO PURCHASE THE BOOK ($10.95 + $2 S&H) OR THE AUDIO TAPE SET ($12.95 + $2 S&H)

CALL: (800)-898-3743

P.A.S.S. C.A.L.F.
8 BEHAVIORS OF SALES SUCCESS IN AN AGRICULTURAL DEALERSHIP

Frank Lee

POWERFUL SALES PROGRAMS FROM SALES ACADEMY, INC.

THE SALES CALL RELUCTANCE® PROGRAM
When well-trained, educated salespeople fail to deliver on the promise sales managers and recruiters forecast for them, it is usually not due to a lack of skill or knowledge. Most times it is due to Sales Call Reluctance® – the emotional short circuit that prevents capable would-be sales superstars from ever reaching their true potential. Even experienced salespeople can suffer the debilitating effects of unresolved cases of Sales Call Reluctance® that put their careers on permanent hold.

SPQ*GOLD™: THE SALES CALL RELUCTANCE® SCALE
Laser-sharp and amazingly accurate, this test identifies the reasons why salespeople do not prospect and provides sales managers and trainers with the tools necessary to better select, develop and manage their salespeople.

THE FEAR-FREE PROSPECTING & SELF-PROMOTION WORKSHOP®
This unique one-day workshop helps salespeople discover and understand how one or more of the 12 types of Sales Call Reluctance® can sabotage their careers. Learn how to manage your fear so it no longer prevents you from making the calls necessary to sustain a successful sales career. All participants receive a Personal Prescription Profile™ that lays out practical ways to beat the Sales Call Reluctance® demon once and for all. Managers learn how to follow up with salespeople to ensure the effectiveness of the workshop.

MANAGEMENT TRAINING WORKSHOP
Sales managers and trainers have called this "the most powerful workshop on earth" for good reason. Unlike any other workshop anywhere, this three-day experience prepares trainers to facilitate the Fear-Free Prospecting & Self-Promotion Workshop® and sales managers to manage salespeople with Sales Call Reluctance®.

SALES CALL RELUCTANCE® STUDIES AND RESEARCH
Sales Academy and Behavioral Sciences Research Press undertake specialized studies and research projects with selected client companies to determine the optimum use of the Sales Call Reluctance® program.

TO FIND OUT MORE ABOUT THE SALES CALL RELUCTANCE® PROGRAM, OR TO PURCHASE ADDITIONAL COPIES OF THIS BOOK, CALL:

(800) 898-3743

POWERFUL SALES PROGRAMS FROM SALES ACADEMY, INC.

SALES TRAINING PROGRAMS

Sales Academy takes a different approach to sales training.Following the principle of the Sales Call Reluctance® program - that most salespeople do not fail because of a lack of skill or ability - Sales Academy looks at developing successful behaviors for salespeople. These are behaviors that propel salespeople to new levels of production.

THE BEHAVIORAL SALES WORKSHOP

In preparation for this workshop, Sales Academy studies the behaviors of a client company's salespeople to identify good and bad selling habits. It then customizes a workshop that teaches salespeople the successful selling behaviors most appropriate for their sales situations. Salespeople learn the value of these behaviors. They also learn practical ways to implement them on a daily basis. Sales managers learn how to manage these behaviors so their salespeople can continue to perform consistently at a higher level.

THE SUCCESSFUL DEALER BEHAVIORS PROGRAM®

Specially developed for the Agricultural Dealership, this is a four- to five-month exercise in developing managers and employees using behavioral models. Everyone in the dealership participates. Managers learn how to develop and implement non-negotiable and successful behaviors in all areas of their dealership. They learn the two essentials of effective management - getting people to do what they should, and developing them to become better. This highly acclaimed program incorporates the Sales Call Reluctance® program, the Behavioral Sales Workshop and the Most Valued Customer/Teamwork workshop.

MOST VALUED CUSTOMER/TEAMWORK WORKSHOP

Practical, hands-on, totally-customized for each dealership. This workshop creates dealership teams to close the gap between what their top customers spend with them and what they spend in total. It also shows how to sytematically acquire additional Most Valued Customers. No theory! Real customers and prospects are chosen. Teams create Strategic Sales Plans in the workshop that they can use the next day.

TO FIND OUT MORE ABOUT THESE SALES TRAINING PROGRAMS, OR TO PURCHASE ADDITIONAL COPIES OF THIS BOOK, CALL:

(800) 898-3743

READER COMMENTS

"If I had the money, I'd buy the rights to this book so it wasn't available to my competition. This is a real nuts and bolts book on how to improve the performance and profitability of the dealer sales department."
Brian Hoven, Hoven Equipment Company, Great Falls, MT.(AGCO)

"This book is a necessary roadmap for properly administrating targets, behavioral expectations and goals. These make sales management fun and rewarding for all involved."
Bob Honzik, Retired Deere Executive

"Good salespeople don't necessarily make good sales managers. If you're like me, a salesperson that was moved into a sales management position and told to hire and manage a sales team, with little or no training, you're going to find Mr. Lee's book a God-send. I would think this is a "must-read guide" for veteran managers and new managers alike as well as a guide for self-motivated and self-employed salespeople."
Craig Pottberg, Ag Sales Manager, Nebraska Machinery Co., Doniphan, NE. (CATERPILLAR)

"The book is easy to read. If one truly commits to following the principles outlined in the book, sales performance is sure to at least improve."
Mark Gettel, Owner, Gettel & Co., Pigeon, MI. (DEERE)

"Is Frank Lee's book the best ever written on Ag sales management? It certainly is the best I have read. If you plan to be in the Ag business 5 years from now, you may want to read this book. Frank Lee has the questions to ask and a model for success."
Bob Hilleque, Senior Instructor, Deere & Co., Minneapolis, MN.

"Frank's book is a simple approach to defining, developing and succeeding at sales management. The simplest things are the hardest to do which is what Frank has outlined in this text book for sales management success."
Todd Stucke, Regional Sales Manager, AGCO, St Henry, OH.

"Frank has written an excellent guide for us and we should use it. Frank, your book can make us better leaders. I am grateful to you for writing it."
Jim Larson, Haug Implement Co., Willmar, MN. (DEERE)

"First, it is a frank, comprehensive account of EFFECTIVE sales management. It provides a concise roadmap that leads a sales manager through all the phases of developing salespeople from recruitment to training to gaining full potential! I especially liked how the essentials of work ethic, integrity, trust and consistency are stressed in the process. These qualities allow the sales manager, working in conjunction with the dealership owner, to be the catalyst that spreads the right kind of culture throughout the dealership that ultimately delivers GENUINE VALUE to customers"
Jim Milstead, Branch Manager, Deere & Co., Reno, NV.

"I would describe the reading as a meticulously documented composition for the success-oriented sales manager who is willing to inaugurate and implement decision-making policies that complement the integrity of his or her organization in all situations."
Ron Tiller, Regional Sales Manager, Woods Equipment Co., TN.

"This book is a very complete and thorough summary of the sales manager's roles and responsibilities at a successful ag dealership. It provides an outstanding "back to the basics" description of the position. Every sales manager should review this book to provide a self assessment of his own job performance".
Doug Griffin, Ag Dealer Development Manager, Caterpillar Inc.

"Frank Lee CARES about the sales managers he writes for. Skill after skill, tip after tip, his intent is clear - that sales management is a profession that can be nurtured and practiced to great success. Sales managers in the Ag industry now have an invaluable working manual that is written lovingly for them by a consummate insider."
Ong Hock Seng, KnowledgeVentures, Singapore

"Frank's book is extremely well written. It will absolutely help any dealer improve on sales and the sales performance of the salespeople."
Dean Barnard, North American V.P. of Sales, AGCO Corp.